As one of my mentors ~~responsible for pushing me~~ days at the start of my entre~~ ~~ now resulted in a multi-si~~ ~~ the importance of having a~~ ~~ guidance myself, I couldn't recommend ~~..~~ Strategy and the SellerPro Academy enough – t~~he~~y without a doubt the best *Amazon* FBA training resources in the world right now.'

– JORDAN PLATTEN
Author of the 15 Minutes Agency

Jonny is an absolute champion when it comes to branding and creating products and services that truly serve their customers. His eye for detail and ability to communicate this through his programs and training are extraordinary. If you're looking to learn how to create a product that'll stand out and become a huge success, then you need to be learning from Jonny. There is no one better.

– Ed J C SMITH
Author of Money Mindfulness and Founder of the Champion Academy

For anyone who wants to dominate e-commerce, Jonny is the man. I'm in the process of launching a high-end lingerie company and, although personal branding is my zone of genius, it's a totally different ball game when it comes to e-commerce. He got me to think about how I want my customers to feel when they buy and wear my products, and that has helped me totally change how I'm doing to marketing and promote everything.

LAUREN TICKNER
Founder of the Impact School Podcast

To get me to sit down for a prolonged period of time is nearly impossible. However, Jonny's SellerPro Academy and his One Product Strategy are so good, I actually finished them in record time. I recommend few courses, but I have no problem recommending this one. It the best *Amazon* FBA training out there.

IMAN GHAZH
CEO *of IAG Media*

I knew I wanted to start my own business, and knew I had the ability to do so, however, my mindset was completely off. Through working with Jonny, I have learned how to be a business owner and, more importantly, how to act with urgency and always focus on high-quality results. I'm more successful than I'd ever thought was possible, and a lot of this is due to the lessons I learned from Jonny.

WILLIAM RICHARDS
Owner of In A Nutshell Creative

Jonny took a chance with me. I had to drop out of university when I began his mentorship to pursue my passion for entrepreneurship. He steered me down a path to master a high-value skill and has helped me scale my business while creating a huge network through his own knowledge and experience of starting an affluent career.

DAN PRIOR
CEO *of Luxury Vault*

I reached £10K in sales just two months after launching my first product on *Amazon*. Since then, I've been consistently making over £5,000 in sales per month for an initial investment of under £1,000! I'm preparing myself to scale up in the coming months. Overall, I'm really happy with my progress so far. A massive thank you to you, Jonny.

MICHAEL M
SellerPro Academy Member

I started *Amazon* to break free from the rat race and become financially free. I was 22 and a manager at a bank earning around 35k a year (not bragging!). It seemed great at first until you realise you are still in the rat race no matter how much you work your way up. Not only is the course massively in-depth, but Jonny's help is invaluable!

ANT S

SellerPro Academy Member

Just wanted to say a massive thank you for all your support so far. It makes such a difference going through the process knowing that someone has your back all the way, and you really gain confidence by going through the course. Learning about FBA has changed everything for me already, and it's only the beginning! Thank you so much.

ELLA S
SellerPro Academy Member

Jonny, like a sports coach, knows how to keep you motivated when the going gets tough and you want to quit. His training and support groups are thorough and complete enough to get me, a complete beginner in e-commerce, started onto a journey that I can't imagine not being a part of anymore.

GREG L
SellerPro Academy Member

Jonny's course has been invaluable in learning all about Amazon FBA. He comes across as someone who is passionate about helping others succeed, and the support is incredible!

PAUL H
SellerPro Academy Member

What Jonny has set up is a community which allows others to be inspired by those on the same journey! The experience I have had speaking to Jonny has been second to none. His desire to see others succeed displays the type of character he is. Thank you for your constant support.

Saif C
SellerPro Academy Member

After looking for some time for an online business opportunity, and watching countless videos, I am so happy that I bought SellerPro Academy! Jonny's guidance & support is second to none and he is always accessible and gets back to you - the best FBA course & the best FBA coach!

TINA C
SellerPro Academy Member

I found he explains the modules step by step with an easy to understand terminology without the jargon. I'm a complete beginner his approach has helped me enormously to build confidence in myself believing I can do this. I will be recommending Jonny to my friends and family. Thank you, Jonny.

LIZ M
SellerPro Academy Member

THE

ONE

PRODUCT

STRATEGY

JONNY BRADLEY

DISCLAIMER

This book is for educational purposes only. The author and publisher are not offering it as legal, accounting, or other professional services advice. The views and opinions expressed are those of the author alone and also not that of any referenced companies including JungleScout, Google and Amazon. The reader is responsible for his or her own actions. Adherence to all applicate laws and regulations, including international and local governing professional licensing, business practices, advertising and all other aspects of doing business in the United Kingdom or any other jurisdiction is the sole responsibility of the purchaser or reader. Neither the author nor the publisher assumes any responsibility or liability whatsoever on the behalf of the purchaser or reader of these materials. Although the author and publisher have made every effort to ensure that the information in this book was correct at the time, the author and publisher do not assume and hereby disclaim any liability to any party for and loss, damage, or disruption caused by errors or omissions, whether such errors or omissions results from negligence, accident, or any other cause.

DEDICATION

To my amazing partner, family and friends, you are my inspiration and the reasons why I do what I do. You've all supported me when I was struggling to become an entrepreneur, and I can't thank you enough for your love and support that helped me push through.

To my incredible team, I wouldn't have achieved nearly anywhere near as much without all of you. Thank you for your immense loyalty and dedication towards serving our clients.

To my clients, none of this would exist without you. No one would be listing, and no one would care. Thank you for all your support and trust in me. I cannot thank you all.

CONTENTS

01

HOW MONEY MADE ME HAPPY

For me, the day was a complete write-off ... I'd messed up and had only myself to blame.

It was one of those days, you know the ones, where *someone* or *something* has pissed you off, and you've been running it through your mind over and over, wishing there was some magic way to turn back time.

It all started when my internet went down. You may think... "Jonny, first world problems mate, get a grip" However my entire business is built around access to the internet and there are only two things that *really* piss me off:

- Slow (or no) internet

- Traffic

In essence I hate my time being wasted by things out of my control and even more than that... I hate wasting my own time because of thing inside my control.

On this day I had an extremely important presentation to deliver, the presentation wasn't finished, I wasn't fully prepared and then... *Boom*. The internet went down and I flipped. Getting physically angry and hitting the desk with the bottom of my closed fist. I could feel my blood boiling and my stress level went from 0-100 in a matter of minutes.

Looking back on it I feel embarrassed actually telling you this story as in hindsight it seems like such a non-issue however, at the time it felt like my life was ending.

I needed a solution and *Starbucks* was the answer. Good old trusty *Starbucks* would be my saviour: Free internet and coffee.

Packed my laptop into my bag, jumped into the car and left.

Enter the second thing that triggers me like you wouldn't believe: Traffic.

It was about 11AM, and for some unknown reason as soon as I got onto the main road, complete standstill traffic. I was hitting the steering wheel, swearing under my breath and as 20 minutes went by, I was about to blow a gasket. It's funny, writing this I'm starting to get the same feeling as I relive that day, so I better finish this story quickly before I ruin the entire book!

Somehow, I mean, *I have no idea how*, I didn't implode. I arrived, ordered my drink and sat down. When I started working, trying to finish this presentation, I couldn't. My mindset had been flipped on its head and now I was in no mood to work. In fact, the work I did do was probably the worst I've ever done.

I made an executive decision to finish my drink and just head home. I cancelled the presentation, arriving home I turned on TV and sat in-front of it for the next 7 hours.

The crazy thing is that although I had had the worst day I'd had in a long time, I had still made well over £1,000 from my *Amazon* store – without lifting a finger, without spending any time on it, and without thinking about it *at all*.

When I checked my sales at the end of the day lying in bed and blurry eyed, those totals put a smile on my face. I remembered that making money made everything better. Money truly made me happy,

I know...I'm triggering you right now.

Can money buy happiness?

Does money make me truly happy?

Will money make you happy?

You've probably heard these questions answered with a firm, 'NO, it doesn't!' But is that the case?

At that moment, yes, money had made me happy. Not because of the amount, but because I didn't have to work for it. This is what I want you to feel. I want you to experience how incredible it feels when you update your sales dashboard and realise that you've made hundreds, maybe even thousands, of pounds while you were riding a Ferris wheel at Winter Wonderland in Hyde Park after drinking far too many glasses of mulled wine.

Of course, money itself doesn't provide happiness; it's more the opportunities that money allows you to have that make you happy. It's up to you what you decide to do with those opportunities. Maybe you'll use the extra cash to pay off your home or take an exotic vacation. Or maybe you'll use it to put a deposit down on your first home or simply make sure your bills are paid each month. Or maybe you'll build an empire one product at a time.

In this book, I am going to share some of my closely guarded secrets for selling on *Amazon* and specifically how to create a bestselling product and brand – with what I call my 'One Product Strategy'.

This is the exact same strategy I teach to my paying clients, the same strategy that has generated well over £1.5 million worth of sales for my clients in just the last 12 months.

If you finish only one book this century, let it be this one!

At the end of the book, you will have two choices: start your own business or don't start your own business. It's as simple as that.

You will either want to make money or not; there's no in-between. If you find yourself stuck in the middle, get down off that fence and pick a side! No one ever made money while sitting undecided on the fence!

WHAT YOU DO WANT TO HEAR ...

There's never been a better time to start your own online *Amazon* business. Over the next few pages, you're going to learn about the strategies that make selling on *Amazon* the greatest business model in the world and the reasons why I got involved – and why many of my clients do as well.

By reading this book you're going to fully understand why customers buy the things they do, and once you understand why customers make the decisions, they do you can actually predict their behaviour and insert your product at exactly the right time.

You'll be able to create incredible, *no-brainer* product offers that customers line up to buy. The lessons you'll learn will show you how to get exponentially more customers than ever before, not because of some sales or marketing trick, but because they can't help but buy your product.

Finally, you're going to learn techniques that 99% of sellers or even business owners don't know so ultimately you can become experts in e-commerce. I want you to dominate your competition, create brands that change the world, and this is where you're going to start.

Of course, reading this book will not guarantee you any results as for every success story you'll learn about there's a great deal of work that's gone in to making it happen and you have to be willing to put in that same dedication to your own success to make it a reality.

I have been fortunate enough to teach thousands of people these skills, so the lessons you're going to learn have been crafted and optimised to be as efficient as possible.

WHAT YOU DON'T WANT TO HEAR ...

Many people believe that starting a company is hard work ... they're right! Sorry.

It's true that starting a business is hard work – of course it is. Nothing worthwhile was ever easy, right?

However, this doesn't mean that it isn't simple. The strategies you will learn are, in essence, simple. But it's how you as a person implement those same strategies that really makes the difference between success and failure.

You have to really want it; you can't 'sort of' want it!

Are you ready to start?

I'll assume you said 'yes'.

Before I get going, you may be thinking, 'Is this book for me?' If so, let me tell you who this book is for, so there's no confusion.

If you're working that job you don't like and you're looking for a way to build a business in your spare time because you're sick of making your boss richer while wishing you could create something for yourself... then this book is for you.

If you've tried your hand at business before but it didn't work and now you've afraid of failing again and you wish that you had a step by step strategy to get you to the place you want to be... then this book is for you.

If you're sick of doing the same thing every day and

you want to do something that engages your creativity and allows you to build a brand that your customers can love... then this book is for you.

The crazy thing is that most sellers on Amazon don't know what you're about to learn. If you've never sold on Amazon, then what I'm about to tell you will blow your mind.

02

HOW DOES THE ONE PRODUCT STRATEGY ACTUALLY WORK?

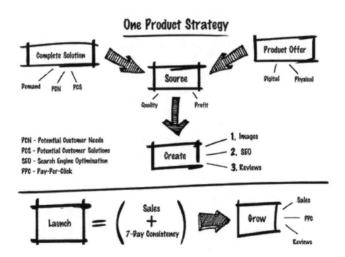

One Product Strategy

Complete Solution — Demand, PCN, PCS

Source — Quality, Profit

Product Offer — Digital, Physical

PCN - Potential Customer Needs
PCS - Potential Customer Solutions
SEO - Search Engine Optimisation
PPC - Pay-Per-Click

Create
1. Images
2. SEO
3. Reviews

Launch = (Sales + 7-Day Consistency)

Grow
Sales
PPC
Reviews

For a long time, I tried to create one formula that shows exactly the process my clients and I were following. A system that took something complex and presented it in its simplest form without losing any of its unique points. I love equations so much, I have them tattooed on my body. I believe they give you ultimate simplicity in a world of chaotic activities .

My favourite equation is $[\Delta_\chi \Delta_\rho \geq \frac{\hbar}{2}]$ which, at first glance, looks like just shapes and letters, but this is called the 'Heisenberg's Uncertainly Principle'. It states that the velocity and position of a particle cannot be measured exactly, even in theory (Encyclopaedia Britannica). Basically, it means that the more you know about an object's position the less you know about its velocity; and, the more you know about its velocity, the less you know about its position. In essence, it is 'uncertain', meaning that you can never, ever know where anything is at any time. An odd thought, but I love it.

I've been fascinated with science and quantum physics since I was very young, so loved finding an equation that made the complex topic of creating a success of selling on *Amazon* very simple.

For months, I mean months and months, I tried to do it. I kept coming back to the idea that if someone can make sense of the universe in a few symbols and letters, why the hell can't I make sense of selling on *Amazon*?

One day, after 50 or so scrunched up pieces of paper, I drew this scribble:

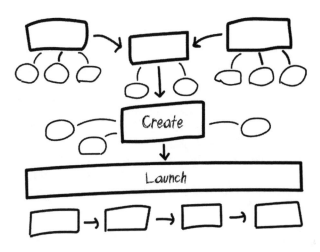

A few hours later, that one scribble turned into the strategy as I know it now.

Suddenly it all fell into place and seemed so obvious. It reminded me of a quote:

> *"True simplicity is, well, you just keep on going*
> *and going until you get to the point where you go,*
> *'Yeah, well, of course.' Where there's no rational*
> *alternative."*

Jony Ive (USA Today).

I had finally captured what made my system unique and had scribbled on a piece of paper just how my students would get the crazy results they get now.

WHY DOES THE STRATEGY WORK?

Don't just take my word for it. Here are two case studies from two of my clients who have used the one-product strategy.

Emilian launched his first product in mid-2018, and within six months, he was selling around £30,000 per month. A year on, he is doing upwards of £68,000 in sales per month. This growth is incredible, and he thanks me all the time. He was thanking me, but I was saying that it was he that put in the hard work, and I was just a catalyst to give him that kick start.

He said, 'From one click to your video to £250,000 profit a year' all this comes from just one product.

Just one product ...

Now, Emilian really understand what it takes to create a close to seven-figure company with one product, so now he can replicate that success with product number two.

Some of you may be thinking that he should have launched a second product by now. However, by the end of this book, you're going to understand why he didn't do it, and more importantly, how he got to where he is today.

Janson is another student who had life changing results. He is an integral part of our community, always willing to help others, and that's exactly what I love about our community – we're all there to push each other forward.

Janson's success is another prime example of what you can achieve when you focus on just one product at a time. Janson generated £33,230 in sales in just 30 days, and the crazy thing is that he only started selling three to four months prior.

Janson has a full-time job in central London which

he plans to keep while he continues to scale his *Amazon* business which just goes to show that you can work an extremely demanding, full-time job and still find the time to have a business that makes multiple six-figures per year.

So, now that you know it works, I'll move on.

To make it as simple as possible for you to learn the strategy, I've broken it up into five main steps. Each step will have numerous points and sub-strategies so that you can implement them in the most efficient and effective way possible. Here they are:

1. DISCOVER

2. SOURCE

3. CREATE

4. LAUNCH

5. GROW

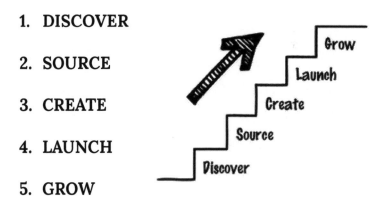

If you need a mnemonic device to remember the steps just say, "**D**oing this **S**trategy **C**an **L**ead to **G**rowth.

03

HOW THE MAN THAT STANK OF FISH CHANGED MY LIFE

M y name is Jonny Bradley, and I'm an entrepreneur from the UK. Previously, I thought that having a job was the only way to become successful. I've always been entrepreneurial, just never been any good at it.

For years I have worked for big corporations, most notably *Apple*. For five years, I consumed their ethos and swallowed it down every day. While I love the company, I was there for far too long. I started just after I finished university and became an 'Expert' (their term not mine) in sales. I was their Sales Trainer responsible for training, teaching, mentoring, and educating not just the sales team but every member of the nearly 100-person-strong workforce.

I was fortunate enough to see behind the curtain of one of the most successful companies in the world, and I understood how they communicated their ethos; their 'Credo', to every team member and customer. This went on for a while, and every now and again, I'd get a leadership role or a secret trip to Apple HQ – it seems fancy, but really, that's just what they do all the time.

It got to the point where I was working at 300% every day, starting early and staying late, just for an insulting pay raise at the end of the year. There were no bonuses; just a 'thank you' and a single-figure-percentage pay increase that only just covered inflation.

I finally left for a real sales job and quickly realised that most companies have no idea what they're doing when it comes to sales, strategy, and keeping their workers happy.

I quit that job and moved to London thinking that this was how I'd become minted. I bought the very finest 'Primark' suit and started working in central London.

This just wasn't me, and after commuting for three hours a day in a sweat-filled, fart-infused train, it started to slowly eat away at me. I felt unfortunately that my frown would not be turning upside-down any time soon.

I remember one day when I was working late (which was expected), and I went to get the train home. It was a pretty normal day, but the train was packed because of a strike – great. Worse than that, the man next to me stank, I mean STANK, of fish. Now, I'm no fan of the fishmonger in the supermarket at the best of times; smoothly swerving down the next aisle while not breathing is one of my fortes. This, however, was what can only be described as 'nostril vomit'.

I'd had enough of this, and I started looking at ways to make more money, at the very least so I could get a faster train or an *Uber* once a week. I started researching ways to make money online, much like you've probably done, and eventually I stumbled across selling on *Amazon*. It looked pretty cool, but scary – oh so scary. There was stock, branding, tax, listing, and advertising to consider. It seemed like a lot of work, especially for me when I'm out of the house by 7 a.m. and not back until around 8–9 p.m. I'll decided I'd leave it at that.

This all changed when I was on holiday a few months later.

I had pulled together enough money to go to Turkey, in the off season, just after a horrific shooting you may remember. No one wanted to go to Turkey. As a result, 5-Star hotels were dirt cheap which suddenly brought them into my price range. I was straight in there (you could say like swimwear). I booked everything, and off my girlfriend and I went.

During the first week, I read a few mindset-type books and consumed hours of *YouTube* content. In the second week, I made a decision that would change my life as I knew it and, importantly, the lives of the people around me. That one decision would get me ten times my current income in 12 months and more than twenty times that over the next two years. That one decision allowed to me positively impact thousands of people and led me to write this book for you, hoping to change your life for the better as well.

So now, I'll bet you're thinking that I'm just going to say, 'Start selling on *Amazon*' and, although yes, I did make that decision, that was not the decision that made the difference. The decision I made and the epiphany I had was this: I decided that I could not succeed if I did not go balls deep (for those of you that are wondering how deep that is, let me tell you ... it's deep), and on the other hand, I would not let myself fail by giving up .

I made myself a promise that I was going to focus all my attention on starting my new business. I wasn't going to go out drinking. I was going get up early and go to bed late just to find that extra 30 minutes to work on my side hustle. I was going to slack off at work and go home on time regardless of whether they wanted to fire me. I was going to sacrifice time with my loved ones now so that I could spend more time with them in the future.

Just like the Karate Kid, *I was going to fight so I didn't have to fight again.*

The day after I returned to the UK, I decided to enroll in an online course. This was one of the scariest things I have ever done. Spending money on my own development seemed like it might be throwing money away. How things have changed – now I will happily pay for knowledge, experience, or mentorship if it will save me time and make me money! Don't you just hate it how much hindsight is 20/20?

The act of paying for training was influential as I was not in a financial situation where I could afford to lose. I *had* to make it work; I *had* to be a success. I couldn't face the embarrassment of giving up as have I had done before. I was pumped up, scared, and excited about what was to come next.

So why am I telling you this story? I want to show you that there is only one thing that matters – and that is *you*.

You decide to be successful, and *you* decide to fail.

You are 100% in charge of your life, of the decisions you make, and how you react to situations both in and out of your control. To be successful, *you* must take ownership of your actions, successes, and failures. Make the commitment right now that you're going to start to take action. Make a commitment to the success of *your own future*.

The simple act of making a commitment – verbal, mental or written – is profound.

When I made this commitment, my fear of failure diminished, and my vision for the future augmented (that's right, my thesaurus game is strong).

Before I move on, my aim for you is simple: to provide you with the highest quality knowledge and show you why selling on *Amazon* is one of the best business models in the world. I am going to show you how you can create a bestselling brand with no experience, no technical knowledge at all, and a small budget – all with just one product.

What I want you to do now is use the next page to write out your 'why' and what you will do when you have your business successfully up and running. But also, what would happen if you don't take action, how will your life change if you continue to stay doing the same thing.

WHAT IS YOUR 'WHY?'

_____

_____

_____

_____

_____

_____

_____

HOW WOULD STARTING A SUCCESSFUL BUSINESS CHANGE YOUR LIFE?

_____

_____

_____

_____

_____

_____

_____

WHAT HAPPENS IF YOU DON'T TAKE ACTION?

_____

_____

_____

_____

_____

04

3 REASONS WHY YOU'LL FAIL AND 3 WAYS TO OVERCOME THEM

A few years ago, I started up a company, spent two years planning, spent thousands on it, and it failed miserably because ... well actually because of a combination of all three failure points you're going to hear about. But mainly it failed because the product just wasn't good enough. Customers didn't really want it.

At the time I thought that the service was innovative, revolutionary and would make me extremely successful. I started learning everything I needed, hiring people to do the website, getting investments to start the company and it was the only thing I was focusing on at the time, My evenings, my mornings and my weekends all revolved around starting this business.

My best friend at the time was a 50% owner of the business and the subsequent issues drove a wedge between us. The business was already failing, losing money every month and I made a call to my friend and business partner. The purpose of the call was to draw a line and close the company, to pay back our loan and go our separate ways. However, when it came down to the money and how we were going to pay back the thousands of pounds we'd borrowed, he decided that there was nothing legally that said he personally had to pay back the money.

It gets worse because we borrowed the money from my family, so he was telling me that he was not willing to pay back my family after they'd supported him through his dream of starting a company. You can imagine, I was not best pleased, and I believe his true colours showed. I said to him, "Take the day to think about what you've just told me. If you want to reconsider then call me tomorrow, if not then this will be the last time I ever speak to you."

That phone call happened in early 2017 and I have not spoken a single word to him since. Just a few weeks later I started up my new business selling on *Amazon*, I paid back the loan in full to my family and I quit my job becoming the full-time entrepreneur I've always wanted to be.

All this could have been avoided if I understood why businesses failed and how to overcome them.

This issue is big in the business world, but in this book, you're going to learn about a strategy that means you will never sell a product that customers don't want. You're not going to spend two years planning just for it to fail and lose your friends, and you won't have to invent anything at all.

You can start so many different types of businesses, many that will make you a boatful of cash. However, according to the Bureau of Labor Statistics' Business Employment Dynamics the shocking truth is that 20% of businesses fail in the first year and 50% within the first five years.

As an entrepreneur, you are embarking on a journey of development, and I know that you'll be feeling a lot of uncertainty about the future. This is normal and, regardless of what figures you look at, you'll be nervous because you never know what the future holds. In general, businesses fail for three reasons:

- Bad Product;

- Not Enough Customers;

- Not Scalable.

FAILURE POINT 1: BAD PRODUCT

How many times have you been sitting at the pub or with friends and someone says, 'I've got this great idea ...' and then go on to tell you about their business or product idea? One of two things usually happen. One: It's a terrible idea. Two: It's a great idea, but they will never make it happen. Very rarely is there a third outcome. Quite often people try and think about how they can invent a product or service, but this mostly leads to failure because the product is bad, or it never sees the light of day. The problem is that most business owners spend thousands on setting up their companies and planning for years to then launch a product that no one wants.

Can you imagine spending all that time and money on something that fails because it's a bad product?

In the next chapter you'll learn how to find the best products to sell that you know customers will love, so having a bad product will never be an issue you face!

FAILURE POINT 2: NOT ENOUGH CUSTOMERS

Have you ever been walking down your local high street and seen a store that's closed down? You see stores opening and closing all the time and sometimes it comes down to one fact: Most companies fail for the very simple reason that they just can't get enough customers. It's really as simple as that – they don't make any money even if they have a great product. The saying goes, 'The more people that know about you, the more buy from you'.

On the other hand, *Amazon* are now the largest online retailer of all time. I know that *Amazon* is an extremely well-funded leader in its field with zero signs of slowing.

- Just last year (2018) they grew their revenue by over 30%;

- This made them the eighteenth most profitable company in the world;

- They have over 6,000 online sales per minute.

The key part for you is that *Amazon* already has the customers, and they are spending billions every year acquire more. You'll never have the issue of not having enough customers when selling through *Amazon* and the even more important thing is that they are growing, so if it seems like a lot now, just wait as it will only grow.

FAILURE POINT 3: NOT SCALABLE

Another reason companies fail is because they aren't scalable. I'm not sure if you're aware, but scaling a company, hiring employees and everything that comes along with it is not easy and can cost a fortune. Wouldn't it be incredible if you could just tap into *Amazon*'s existing system of logistics, customer support, and online strategy?

That is exactly what Fulfilment by *Amazon* (FBA) does for you. It's my favourite part of the how this business works as it allows you to sit back and have hundreds, even thousands, of employees, a world-leading tech team, and a fulfilment system to hold and ship your products without even logging onto your computer. All this is 100% done for you.

If you want to sell more products – easy. If you want to sell fewer – easy. There are no diseconomies of scale when it comes to fulfilment, staffing, tech, etc., as *Amazon* has all of that handled for you. They have the headroom to grow as you do, they can adapt to your exact business needs, and, let me tell you, for someone who had a failed business for this very reason, this is just an incredible system. Do not underestimate it.

Now that you understand why companies fail let's jump into the One Product Strategy with the first two stages:

- The Complete Solution;

- The Product Offer.

05

FINDING PRODUCTS TO SELL THAT YOUR CUSTOMERS WILL LOVE.

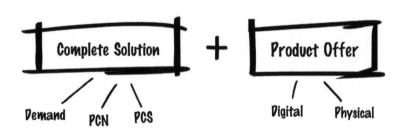

Have you ever seen a horse wearing black plastic flaps next to each eye? These are called 'blinders', and their purpose is to prevent a horse from seeing what's behind and beside them, so they don't get distracted or panic.

That's sort of like what every guru out there is doing with product research. They are fitting their students and followers with blinders by telling them that there are really only two things to worry about when doing product research: first that there have to be 'high sales', and second that there has to be 'low competition' for when you're doing your product research.

While these two metrics are important, imagine if you were to remove the blinders so you could start seeing the true opportunity that's out there.

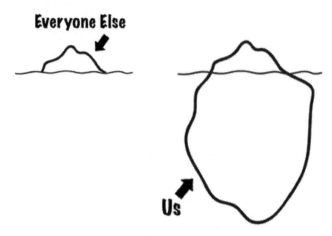

By only looking at the tip of the iceberg , you will disregard products that have an exceptional earning potential just because the numbers weren't in the 'Goldilocks Zone'. By following the Product Discovery Strategy I'm about to teach you, you will find hidden treasures while everyone else is only seeing 10% of what's out there.

WHAT IS PRODUCT DISCOVERY?

Product Discovery:

- The discovery of products through research and analysis. In short, I call this 'The Complete Solution';

- Strategic creation of an irresistible Product Offer.

By using these two techniques, you will research and analyse the data along with assessing the true needs of your customers which will allow you to create incredible product offerings. If you implement this strategy, you'll stand out from the crowd of other sellers, your costs will go down, and your profit margin will go up!

IT ALL STARTS WITH 'THE COMPLETE SOLUTION'

When I worked for Apple, I learned about something called the 'Complete Solution.' It was the theory behind offering the customer the full range of products so they can walk away with everything they need on the day. The key was that the solution was 'Complete' and the customer wouldn't need to go anywhere else to get the result they wanted.

All I had to do was adapt this formula for selling on *Amazon*. I started working on how I could create products that when a customer buys them, they get everything they needed delivered to them the next day. There are three main components to the Complete Solution, so let's go through each of them now.

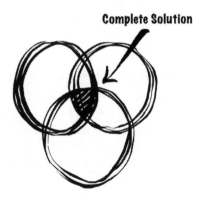

Complete Solution

It all starts with 'Demand'. You need to first find products that sell – no shock there.

Most companies fail because they can't get enough customers. On *Amazon*, this can happen if you choose a product with low demand as it means that not enough people are searching for and buying the product. This is sort of like opening a hairdressing salon on a polar ice cap. You're not going to be cutting any hair there anytime soon as there is no demand for the service.

However, open that same hairdressers on a busy high street, and you'll probably have a successful business as there are more customers there who want the service. It's really as simple as that. So, you have to find products to sell that already have people searching for them every day and, importantly, buying them every day.

WHAT ARE YOU LOOKING FOR?

Here's the thing, the data I'm about to share with you will change over time, so in the interest of making this book as relevant as possible, I'm going to give some broad figures. Depending on your geographic location, these numbers will also vary. However, once you understand WHY you are using these numbers, then you can easily adapt to your circumstances.

STEP 1: FIND THE BROADEST KEYWORD

When you go on *Amazon* and you want to find a dog lead, what do you type in the search bar? Most probably would type, 'dog lead'. This is what I would call the 'broadest keyword' or 'broadest search term', meaning it's the simplest word or words you can use to find the product you're after.

Hang on! 'Dog lead' is two words. Surely you can use just 'lead' or 'dog?'

Okay, let's try this. If you search for 'lead', will you only get dog leads? No, you'll get other types of leads, such as power leads or USB Cable. So, that word would be too broad. Equally, you can't search for 'dog' as the search results would also be too broad.

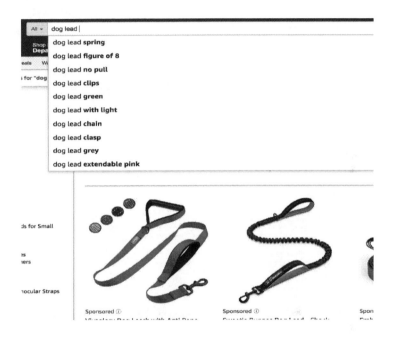

On the other hand, let's say you search 'blue retractable dog lead for large dog'. You'll probably get just dog leads, but most customers do not search like this, and you will not see 90% of the dog leads out there. Most of the time, customers use the simplest and most obvious search terms. When you assess demand, you have to think as a customer would so that when you see the sales and data, you know we're getting the most relevant results. This may sound simple, but you'd surprised by how many people get this wrong, and if you have poor data, you cannot make informed decisions. Think like a customer would and always find the broadest keyword for any product you're researching.

STEP 2: ASSES DEMAND FOR THE FIRST PAGE OF RESULTS

When you search for a product on *Amazon*, you'll be met with the results of that search. If you're a seller with a product on the first page of results and there is demand for the product, you'll be making sales.

Most customers do not look at the second page of results, so your goal is to get your product as close to the front as possible. The closer to page one you are, the more you'll make.

For example, if the top five sellers are all achieving 500 sales per month, but the remaining ten sellers are only making 100 on average, it means that you'd have to be in the top five to be making any sort of income. When you look at the first page, you need roughly 10–12 of those top fifteen sellers to be making good revenue and steady sales. This means that if you get to page one, you'll most likely be making some good cash!

HOW DO YOU KNOW HOW MANY SALES OTHER SELLERS ARE MAKING?

To estimate how many sales any seller or product is making per month, you can use tools to do so, go to www.oneproductstrategy.com/resources to make sure you have the most up to date list of services. The companies and resources on this page are the most trustworthy and accurate tools out there at the moment. All you have to do is:

- Download their extensions for your *Google* Chrome browser;

- When viewing the *Amazon* search results, you hit the extension;

It then pulls in all the data you could ever want, including the number of sales per month/day, number of reviews, FBA fees per product, star rating, and so on...

These tools are estimates and not exact as Amazon does not share exact sales data publicly. They take metrics like the BSR (Best Seller Rank), and then using their advanced algorithms, they estimate how many sales that product will be making per day and per month based upon their BSR.

Amazon Sales Estimator

Our Estimator Tool is a great way to check average monthly sales
numbers for specific Amazon categories, help aid product
launches and a simple way to spy on your competitors.

**Estimated Number of
Sales per Month**   **1,327**

Best Seller's Rank Number ⓘ | 50 |

Amazon Marketplace ⓘ | 🌐 United Kingdom   ▾ |

**Amazon Product Category
Amazon Marketplace** ⓘ | Sports & Outdoors   ▾ |

Clear selection   [Calculate sales!]

For example, if a product in the Sports and Outdoors category has a BSR of 50, they are likely to be making 1,300+ sales per month.

Why do I say 1,300+ rather than 1,327?

Again, these are estimates, and from my own research and analysis, I find most services underestimate sales. I believe this is to safeguard themselves because if they overestimated sales, it could put a lot of people into situations where they aren't able to make the money they were expecting. All they are doing is setting the expectation and it's better to under-promise and over-deliver than to over-promise and under-deliver.

STEP 3: CONDUCT VIABILITY CHECKS

So, you've found a product with great sales and you've assessed the best keywords, and it's all looking great. You go to launch the product when you realise that it's a seasonal product for summer like a paddling pool and you've just bought 500 units at the end of summer. You'd be really surprised how many people completely ignore seasonal trends, fad products, or products that are heavily restricted, then a couple months later, they are in the same position they were in at the beginning.

This will not happen to you because you're going to read this section and you're going to remember it!

There are a few really important checks you have to make. Some products are more complicated than others but here are the three big questions you need to ask yourself:

- is the product *seasonal*?

- is the product *dangerous*?

- is the product a *fad*?

SEASONAL PRODUCTS

These are products where their sales fluctuate based on the season. For example, warm gloves will be seasonal for the winter; in the summer, not many people are buying them. Another example may be Valentine's Day gifts, although not linked to a season as such, their demand is aligned to a holiday, so they will look great in January/ February but come March, everything changes.

There are two ways to check to see if your product is seasonal:

- use common sense;

- use *Google Trends* (www.trends.Google.com).

Google Trends is a great free service where you can type in your broadest keyword, and it'll show you the usage of that keyword over time. I suggest selecting the five-year option so you can see any seasonality very clearly.

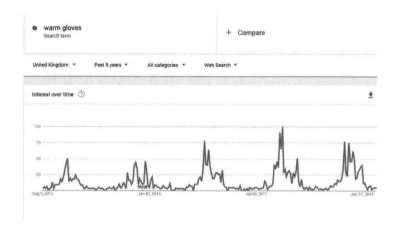

Here is an example of 'warm gloves' which you can clearly see is seasonal.

Here is an example of 'dog lead' which you can clearly see is not seasonal.

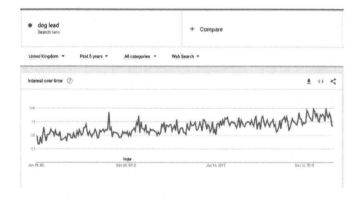

DANGEROUS PRODUCTS

When you hear 'dangerous', you think of things like knives and guns. While yes, you should stay away from any product like those, actually, dangerous products can be, well, not clearly dangerous. An example may be an Electronic Cigarette/Vape Pen. While the sales on these are great, there will likely be issues with local laws, importing, safety concerns, and the potential of laws changing in the future. While you can sell products like this, there will be more hoops to jump through, and you'll have to do more research into local laws regarding the selling of those products. For example, what safety certifications you need, what must be on the packaging, what claims you can and cannot make, etc.

The good thing about products like this is that because they are harder to sell, it means fewer people will actually end up selling them. So, if you don't mind doing the extra legwork and staying patient, then these can be good products to look into. However, don't be deluded into thinking that it's going to be as easy as selling something like a bath towel.

Often these types of products are referred to as 'restricted' which just means *Amazon* places restrictions on sellers before they can sell them. This is to ultimately protect their customers from poor quality or illegal goods. So, if you do it right and you get approval then these, 'dangerous' products can be absolute gold mines! However, for a beginner selling their first product, it would be best to avoid these until you have some more experience.

FAD PRODUCTS

Who remembers Fidget Spinners, the little 3-pronged plastic kids toys that spin in your hand?

This is just one example of a fad product. There have been many more like Loom Bands, YoYo's, Pokémon Cards, Pet Rock, Angry Birds and so on... and there will continue to be many more in the future. While you can make a killing with these fad products at the right time, if you get in at the wrong time, you're screwed.

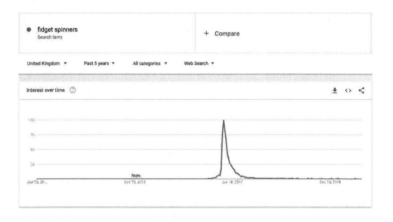

WHY IS IT A GOOD AND HORRIBLE OPPORTUNITY ALL AT THE SAME TIME?

If you look at *Google Trends*, you can see that there is one, ginormous spike around June 2017, a few months before it gathered momentum and then sky rocketed. What happens is that some people who are on the ball see the momentum building and they get in early enough so that they can make huge profits and are there for the demand explosion. However, most people only see the product once it's already too late. They spend weeks negotiating, getting everything sorted, then they order thousands of units, but by the time they arrive in the *Amazon* warehouse, there is even more competition and there's been a price war going on, so now, the profit margin is smaller, and worst of all, they're too late and the demand has peaked and is now on the decline.

With Fidget Spinners, I have friends that were on both sides of that coin – those who hit it early and made a fortune, and those who hit it late and were stuck with thousands of units and no way to sell them.

If you're well-versed in selling on *Amazon*, you have good supplier connections and can see the curve moving up, then you can get involved and take that risk. However, remember that you are getting into a fad product and demand will drop off and profit margins will decrease, so don't get greedy. Just get in and get out! If sellers are all killing it making thousands per day with only a handful of reviews, you're probably already too late!

In my opinion, fad products are good for experienced sellers who can better estimate demand, have the cash flow to order high volumes, and have an exit strategy so they aren't left with excess stock. Fad products are bad for first-time sellers who will get a little overzealous and end up really making bad decisions. Often, I've seen people so eager to start selling that they either ignore the facts or they just don't even bother to check. If you do the research, you'll have a far higher chance of success. Remember this is the One Product Strategy, not the "Start one product, fail, try again before you eventually give up Strategy."

THE COMPLETE SOLUTION: PART 2

So now you have found a product (or products) that meets your demand criteria; this was the first step in creating a complete solution. As I mentioned before, most gurus will now tell you to go and sell that product. You're about to learn what 99% of *Amazon* sellers don't know, to do this, you need to find out the Potential Customer Needs.

Over the next few pages, I'm going to teach you a trick for how I do this repetitively, but first you should understand the reasons people are most likely to buy.

TOWARDS PLEASURE/AWAY FROM PAIN

Think back to the last time you bought something online; What was it?

For me, it was a replacement water pump for a cat fountain; Yes, you heard that right. Search for it on *Amazon* if you don't believe they exist.

Think about the product and ask yourself these questions:

- why did I spend my hard-earned money on this product?

- did I buy it to get away from a pain point?

- did I buy it to get pleasure in some way?

There are two primary reasons you purchase a product:

Towards Pleasure / Away From Pain

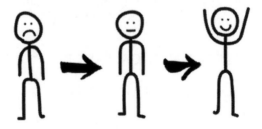

- it will help you get away from some sort of pain;

- it will help you get some sort of pleasure.

Let me give you an example of each using my cat fountain pump.

AWAY FROM PAIN:

- the current pump stopped working so needed replacing;

- the cats only drink from running water, so without the fountain, they don't have anywhere to drink from;

- cats will become dehydrated if I don't buy a replacement fountain or get a new pump;

- having a cat fountain means I don't have to replace water every day, saving myself time;

- I often forget to fill up water bowls, so this is better, and it holds more water;

- water bowls gather lots of dust and cat hair in the water so get dirty quickly.

TOWARDS PLEASURE

- it's amusing when you see a cat drinking from a fountain;

- not having to top up water every day saves me time, which is great, as I often forget simple tasks;

- I know that the cats will stay hydrated, especially on hot days;

- the cats enjoy drinking and playing with the water ... happy cat = happy owner;

- buying just the pump means I can save money as I

don't need to buy an entire fountain.

Now, think about that product you just bought and do the same thing. Think about the two sides of the same coin. How did buying the product move you away from pain and/ or towards pleasure?

Use the activity on the next couple of pages to start this process using two products you've recently purchased.

PRODUCT:

_____

_____

_____

_____

_____

_____

_____

AWAY FROM PAIN:

_____

_____

_____

_____

_____

_____

_____

TOWARDS PLEASURE:

_____

_____

_____

_____

_____

_____

PRODUCT:

_____

_____

_____

_____

_____

_____

AWAY FROM PAIN:

_____

_____

_____

_____

_____

TOWARDS PLEASURE:

_____

_____

_____

_____

_____

_____

DESIRE

People buy things because they desire a result.

- if you purchased this book, you may desire your own successful business;

- if you hire a personal trainer, you may desire an athletic physique;

- if you buy a memory foam pillow, you may desire a better night's sleep.

Your ultimate goal in creating your product and brand is to help your customers, to provide them with a solution they are going to love. To do this, you need to understand exactly what would make them love it. What is it that your customers desire? What end results are they after?

If you're selling a product but you don't know what your customers actually want, how on earth are you going to create something that truly helps them achieve it?

There are two elements that make up desire:

- what results do they want?

- what results do they not want?

Desire can be just as much about what people do *not* want than what they do, for example;

- if you got this book, you may desire to not be in debt for the rest of your life;

- if you get a personal trainer, you may desire to not be in bad shape anymore;

- if you buy a memory foam pillow, you may desire to get rid of your neck ache.

RELATE-ABILITY

Empathy is the ability to share someone else's feelings or experiences by imagining what it would be like to be in that person's situation. You need to have empathy for your customers to really understand their desires and whether they are trying to get towards pleasure or away from pain. Empathy is a competency that you need to get good at. The better you get, the more advanced your product solutions will become. A great way to become empathetic towards your customers is to buy the product and use it yourself.

It's as though I asked you to tell me what it's like to learn the violin. You may be thinking: 'Jonny, I've never learned to play the violin.' If you've never learned to play the violin, then you will have to try really hard to try to imagine what it would be like. You could try to imagine by comparing it to other things you'd done in the past

But what if instead, I gave you a violin and told you to go home and start learning how to play over the next two weeks? Your empathy would be ten times more thorough, you'd really understand what it's like, at that point you are in a far better position to help people who are looking to learn the violin.

Why then, do most people not take this approach when selling on *Amazon*?

If you can't personally use the product, then find someone close to you who can, but never start selling a product yourself if you haven't had either first- or second-hand experience using it.

Here are the punch lines:

- once you understand your customers, you can empathise with their needs.

- once you empathise with your customers' needs, you can understand their desired solutions.

- once you understand their desired solution, you can create the complete solution.

Step One | Step Two

WHAT ARE YOUR CUSTOMERS' TOP NEEDS?

For this exercise you'll need a product idea to work with, if you don't have a product yet, pick a product at random so you can practice this exercise.

Step 1: Get yourself a piece of paper (or use the next couple of pages) and draw a line down the middle.

Step 2: On the left-hand side, write a list of every possible need your customers have. Think about everything we've just gone over – what pain are they moving away from, what pleasure are they moving towards, what do they desire, and what do they not desire. (If you don't have a product yet, pick a product at random so you can practice this exercise)

Step 3: When you think you're done, take a break and then double the size of your list by thinking outside the box until you have a list of around forty points.

Step 4: Take another break.

Step 5: Go back to the list and then on the right-hand side, pull out around five of the most important needs that your customers have. If this ends up being ten, that's okay. The point is to take your entire list and optimise it to include only the best needs, and sometimes this will give you ideas that you'd never even thought of at the beginning.

Step 6: Repeat Steps 5 and 6.

Step 7: You now have your potential customer needs. Congratulations!

THE COMPLETE SOLUTION: PART 3

When you understand your customers, this gets a lot easier, but to stand out from the crowd, you really have to engage what is called your 'subconscious, super-fast brain' (Sedniev, 2013).

Have you ever been in the shower or on the toilet and suddenly you get the answer to a problem that you've been working on for ages? A problem that you were really struggling with, and then suddenly, when you were just minding your own business, it came to you? A glorious epiphany!

Now, I'm going to teach you about the *Vu Jádé* method (Warren Berger). The *Vu Jádé* is a direct result of your subconscious brain working on the problem while you're going about your daily life.

However, it's subconscious, so you can't consciously turn it on and off ... or can you?

When I learned about this method, it changed how I think critically, how I overcome problems, and how I strategise solutions. When you were doing the exercise with the piece of paper split down the middle, when you took breaks, you started to engage your subconscious brain, but to really get it working, you need to forget about the task. You need to take breaks, and that's incredibly important at this stage of the complete solution as with time comes *Vu Jádé*.

WHAT ON EARTH IS VU JÁDÉ, JONNY?!?!?

Vu Jádé is like the opposite of *déjá vu*. In fact, the observant reader will notice it is *déjá vu* reversed. *Vu Jádé* is when you suddenly see something you've seen over and over before, but you suddenly see it in a different way or from a different perspective. When I was creating my HydroFuel

Brand I did exactly what I told you to do in this phase. I had pieces of paper split in two. There were multiple versions of these pieces of paper. I'd tested the product for weeks and weeks, but there was something missing. I was trying to come up with the complete solution, but I just couldn't get there. I couldn't think of a way to really stand out.

And then one day, when I was having lunch at a cafe down the road it hit me. An almost biblical *Vu Jádé* where I saw the same thing I'd been looking at for weeks, but in a totally different light. With HydroFuel, I wanted to help people hydrate as I know that your physical and mental performance has a direct link to your hydration levels. That was my goal, but I couldn't figure out the solution to do it.

MY VU JÁDÉ WAS THIS:

Customers want to be hydrated, but they forget, and then it's too late. They get headaches, and it affects their mood as well and their mental and physical performance. The real issue is that they <u>forget</u> to hydrate. All of the products on the market that try to help just have little graphics on the side of the bottles detailing what times to drink. However, these don't solve the issue if the person isn't looking at the bottle. They still forget, they remain dehydrated, and the issue continues.

However, when you get a phone notification, you look at it. So, to remind people to hydrate, I needed to get my product to where their attention is always focused, and that's when I finished creating my complete solution – a mobile application that sends you notifications throughout the day to hydrate. Each bottle came with a free download, and the app could be tailored and personalised to your weight, activity level, and so on. By implementing this into the solution, I was able to truly help people when they forgot to hydrate which can lead to the headaches, oily skin, and so on.

This *Vu Jádé* allowed me to create a product with a digital element where I could now charge over 30% more than my closest competitor, and my reviews and feedback are incredible as I am actually helping people. If I had launched the product without this, I would not have been able to set a higher price, and my customers would not be as happy.

So, when you're waiting for your *Vu Jádé*, give it time, have patience and let your super-fast subconscious brain do its job!

Now get to get another piece of paper (or use the following exercise pages) and repeat steps 1 through 8 from the previous section, but instead of coming up with potential customer needs, you're going to come up with potential customer solutions.

PEOPLE BUY OFFERS NOT PRODUCTS

Let me ask you this, who wants to go to dinner with me tonight?

Most of you now will be thinking, 'Ooooh, he asked me out' ... I know, I know. Zero people are thinking that.

What you're probably thinking is that it doesn't seem like a good deal, it doesn't seem valuable, and in reality, very few people would actually do this unless they already knew me and wanted my time.

But what if I asked:

Who wants to go to dinner with me tonight? I'll give you all my training for free (normally worth thousands), and I'll mentor you one-on-one for the next three months so you can have all the resources and mentorship that you need to create a successful *Amazon* business. Then, we'll even get ice cream and have a few drinks. All I need you to do is pay £50. How does that sound?

Now, who wants to come?

The £50 price tag seems almost insignificant.

If the cost of a product/service is more than the perceived value, then customers do not buy. As soon as perceived value exceeds cost, then customers see a great deal, they get their card out, and they buy.

To sell anything, all you have to do is increase the perceived value so that the perception of cost decreases.

For my first dinner date, the value was low, so most people wouldn't take me up on the offer. But in the second scenario, the perceived value was in the thousands, so the £50 price tag seemed tiny in comparison.

Did the cost change?

No, so what did?

It was your perception of the cost in relation to the value.

The great thing is that this offer doesn't actually cost me anything. I give you training I've already had, I answer a few messages, which costs me nothing, and the only thing left is some ice cream and a bottle of wine.

So, when you're creating your own product offer, it's in your best interests to increase the value as much as you can so that customers go bananas for it.

HOW DO I INCREASE MY VALUE WITHOUT INCREASING MY COSTS?

When I tell people the method I use to increase value to secure more sales and profit, people always say, 'Well surely it must cost more money, so what's the point?', and this is a good thing as this is the attitude of most sellers on *Amazon*. What I'm going to tell you today is that you can do this for extremely low costs, and you can actually make more of a profit because of it. If you ignore this, you're throwing money away and leaving potentially thousands on the table.

There are two ways in which you can increase the perceived value of your product offer: with physical products; with digital products/services.

PHYSICAL PRODUCTS

We all know what a physical product is, at least I hope you do by now. It's a product that you can touch. A great example of how you can increase the value of your product by adding another product is a home workout kit that includes push up bars, abs roller, a yoga mat, and mobility bands. By creating a bundle of products that the customer would need if they wanted to do a home workout, you are essentially saving them the time they would spend finding the products themselves. You can add them into one box and sell together for a higher price point. Yes, it'll cost more to buy the stock, obviously, but you can also charge more because the perceived value is higher.

A simpler example may be as simple as an electronic device where customers keep complaining about the fuse blowing. If you were to include an extra fuse with your product, it becomes more valuable, not because a fuse costs a lot, but because it saves the customer time and a bit of a headache, therefore, the purchase is more valuable to them.

When you're coming up with your complete solution, think about what physical products you can add to your offer that would increase the value of the product for the customer and would genuinely be good for them.

I saw a terrible example of this once when someone emailed after seeing one of my *YouTube* videos. A guy was selling a frying pan but bundled in with that product was a Superman apron. I mean, what on earth were they thinking? This is an example of what not to do. It made zero sense and certainly didn't add any value to the product listing as the customer wanted a frying pan, an example of a suitable bundle could be an oil splatter screen.

When you're creating the physical product offer, here is a little trick you can use to make sure it's right. Create three product offers, each with slightly different items as the additional products but keeping the main product the same. Then find a few people, these can be friends or members of your target demographic, and ask them simply, 'Which one would you buy?'

This is called ... wait for it ... MARKET RESEARCH.

Start asking people which they would buy as you need the opinions from real people. By doing so, you may realise that the offer that you thought was the best one actually isn't perceived as the most valuable and useful. By taking this extra step that hardly anyone else does, you'll end up with a far better product offer than many others simply because you asked ten people.

Don't cut this corner!

DIGITAL PRODUCTS

A digital product is simply a product that is downloadable or accessible on a computer. This can be an eBook, video training, a membership, application or an audiobook. The beautiful thing about digital products is the return on investment (ROI) you get from them. For example, for HydroFuel, I created an eBook with ten recipes for infusing fruit into your water for those that don't like it plain or get bored with the taste of water and want a healthy alternative. And, I give an iOS or Android App that helps them to stay hydrated.

These are both digital product solutions that help the customer based on their needs, but when you spread the cost over the thousands of units that we've sold, the cost is insignificant. The cost is almost zero, but the extra income received is around an extra £4 per unit sold as the value of the product was increased along with the cost to buy, however, the price tag still seems like a great deal because the value is so high. When you compare this to my closest competitor, I am able to charge over 35% more than they do just because of these two digital products that cost almost nothing, which means I am essentially making an extra 35% profit.

This is how powerful digital products can be when used correctly.

Many of you may be thinking that the cost of having an app created is too big, and while, yes, an eBook or training guide is going to be significantly cheaper, but when you work out the cost of the app per unit sold, it's a no-brainer. Unlike physical products, I only have to buy the app creation once.

When you're creating your product offer, I would highly recommend that you think about all the ways in which you can add value by using a digital product and align them to your customers' needs so that it makes actual sense to the customer. Think about how you can add value and create a solution that the customer needs through these digital products. If you do this, you'll be able to make more profit, get more customers, and get better reviews! The goal of the digital product is to help the customer get the most out of the product and to fulfil more of their needs.

I would separate digital products into 3 categories:

- training;

- how-to's;

- community.

Some examples of training would be an eBook, audiobook, or video guide giving the customer educational content around the product or subject. For example, if you had the home workout kit, you could maybe create some home workout training regimes that they can do with the kit.

How-to's can merge slightly with the training, but, like the fruit-infused water recipe book I provide, these can be how to guides on how to get the most out of the product. They can also be care guides or just tips and tricks that will help the customer. The key here is not to create something that has no value. Create something that the customer is actually likely to use.

Lastly, you may want to create a community by inviting customers to a *Facebook* group or something similar. For example, if you were selling in the new-mothers niche, then it would be great if you had a community of new mums whom you can invite your customers to join free of charge. The new mum will find this extremely valuable as they will be able to share experiences with people in the same situation as hers. This doesn't cost you anything at all but will increase the perceived value of your product greatly.

A COMMON MISTAKE WHEN CREATING DIGITAL PRODUCTS

Remember when I told you about the person who wanted my advice regarding their physical bundle of a frying pan and Superman apron? Sometimes people make similar mistakes when creating digital products, like creating an eBook that is completely pointless just because they were told they have to create one. Fortunately for you, many sellers do this. They create poor-quality and irrelevant digital products meaning that when you come along with a high-quality digital product that is super relevant and helpful, you win the fight for clicks, and you gain that customer's business.

The key is to always relate your product to your potential customer's needs.

With HydroFuel, a concern that I found people had with drinking water, specifically tap water, was that they didn't like the taste. While I cannot change the taste of the water that comes out the tap, I can change the taste of it once it's in the bottle. I did this by creating a digital product, in this case, a recipe eBook that contains ten, fruit-infused-water recipes with simple instructions the customer can follow. I tested the recipes and I gave them to my friends, I also made sure the instructions were simple and that they actually tasted good.

Now, I didn't really know if all of my customers would like it, however, I knew that there would be a percentage of customers that don't like the taste of water so are more likely to buy my product rather than the competition even though they can *Google* hundreds of recipes for free. It's because I created a digital product that helped them get away from the pain of not liking the taste of water. This, then, allows me to fulfil my primary brand goal of changing people's hydration habits.

So, when you are creating your own digital product, don't just look at what other sellers do. Instead, think about your customer and what they need, then provide a digital solution to that problem. The more you can help and serve your customers, the more successful you will be, not just selling products, but as an entrepreneur for the rest of your life.

ROUNDUP

Firstly, it all starts with understanding your customers and providing them with a solution that truly serves them. I'm not asking you to reinvent the wheel. Have genuine empathy for your customers as when you understand them, they understand you.

Secondly, take your time as you want to create a product and brand that customers will love, taking a few extra weeks (if needed) to create will always be a worthwhile investment.

Finding Products To Sell That Your Customers Will Love.

06

HOW TO GET THE HIGHEST QUALITY FOR THE LOWEST COST

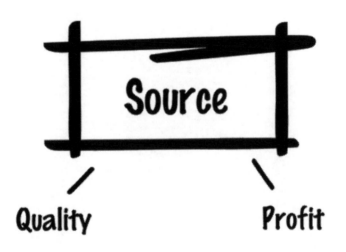

Source

Quality

Profit

S ourcing your product is not just about getting the right price, it's about choosing the right deal, constructing a mutually beneficial relationship with your supplier and understanding the terminology all so you can get the best deal.

There are three focus areas:

- how to become a master negotiator;

- ensuring you always get the best quality products;

- calculating your profit margins so there're no hidden surprises.

HOW TO BECOME A MASTER NEGOTIATOR

I'm not sure about you, but the thought of negotiating isn't a good one for me. I always dreaded this in my previous jobs, and it always made me nervous ... at least that was the case before I learned the skills you're going to learn here.

One thing you have to understand before I move on is that a lot of you reading this will think that you're great at negotiating and you don't need any help at all. Let me tell you, it's very rare to find someone who is great at negotiating, or they think they are great at negotiating when it comes to their day job, but put them in front of *alibaba.com* speaking with manufacturers in China, and suddenly they can't negotiate their way out of a paper bag.

We are going to go through eight of my top tips that will help you through negotiations in your professional and personal life. Then, I'll show you my three-step system for negotiating specifically with manufactures for your product, and by the end of these lessons, you'll be a lethal weapon when it comes to sourcing the best price.

EIGHT THINGS TO KEEP IN MIND

1. NEGOTIATE WITH PURPOSE.

It's often said that margin is made in the negotiations, and this is so true as just a 5% difference in price can make a big impact on your profitability and scalability. Every 1% you negotiate down is another 1% you gain in profit, so you're taking the money out of the manufacturer's pocket and putting it into yours.

2. DETERMINE THE TRUE COST.

The only way to understand what the true cost is (or close to it) is to reach out to multiple suppliers on multiple sites. The more data you have about what everyone is selling the product for, the better informed you'll be when you go to negotiate as you'll know exactly what all the competitors are charging. So, if the supplier you're dealing with gives you a price that's 20% over all others, you know that they have a lot of wiggle room.

3. SPEAK WITH AUTHORITY.

With sourcing, you'll hear a bunch of acronyms and phrases that you'll never hear in normal life, so it's important to have done your research so you know roughly what terms mean. The last thing you want to do is have to ask the supplier what something means. This would be the last resort as you want to show them you know what you're talking about. If you don't know, *Google* it, and if you're in my training programs, go and find out. If a supplier thinks you're new to the game, they will be more likely to take advantage of you, so don't let that slip.

4. BE THE BETTER NEGOTIATOR.

The people you'll be dealing with aren't superheroes in negotiations. Like most, they will be bad, but will have guidelines of what they should and shouldn't say, and what they can do and cannot do. Once you understand that the person you're speaking to is less skilled than you are, you will be able to make some very interesting deals.

5. FOCUS ON QUALITY.

You're not out here to get the cheapest price. Often, the cheapest price equals the lowest quality, however, you know your customers don't want that. What you're looking for is the best value for money compared to the quality. Generally, the higher the quality, the more you can sell the product for. Sometimes, you'll negotiate on other tangibles like bundled products, box printing, two colour logo or one colour. It's not always about price.

6. KEEP YOUR CARDS CLOSE.

Never, under any circumstances, do you say, 'I can only pay a maximum of $4.50 per unit' if $4.50 is actually the highest you can go. This leaves you zero room to negotiate, and also tells them what you're willing to pay. Equally, they would never give their lowest price to you as then you'd expect to get that price, leaving no room for them to negotiate. So, if you know you need to get the product for under $5, then never say that you can only pay up to $5 per unit. Instead, say the most you can pay is $4.00, and you can meet in the middle at $4.50 which makes you look as though you're over budget.

7. HAVE PATIENCE.

The number of times that I've had people say to me, 'Jonny, they just aren't budging on price. What do I do?' Then I ask how long they have been dealing with them and they say, 'Three days'. If you want a great price, you need to have patience and not come off as desperate. Instead of you trying to win them as a supplier, think about it as though they are trying to win you as a customer. Make them work for it, and they will come to you. In other words, 'Treat 'em mean, and keep 'em keen'.

8. PERFECT PRACTICE MAKES PERFECT.

Everyone says, 'Practice makes perfect', however, I disagree as you may be practising doing it wrong! Perfect practice makes perfect. Before you start, learn and understand the terminology. Take training like this and go into it with an action plan. Then repeat the process again and again and again. You don't want your first negotiation to be with the supplier you actually want to do business with as you'll most likely do an awful job. Get some trial runs in just for fun first.

These are tips that you can use in many situations, not just with suppliers, but buying a new car or arguing about who's going to do the washing up.

Always negotiate.

Now that you're set up for success, here is where you go deep.

THREE-STEP SYSTEM FOR NEGOTIATIONS DOMINATION

When implemented correctly, this system is going to do two things for you: save you time and save you money. You'll be able to get to the right price quicker, and that price will be better than you'd ever imagine.

STEP #1: FIND OUT THE LOWEST AND HIGHEST PRICES

As I discussed earlier you need to know the true cost of the product before going all in on one or two suppliers, so how do you do this?

Over hundreds of emails to suppliers and helping thousands of students, I've created a script you can use to start reaching out to suppliers on *alibaba.com.* I love scripts as they not only save time, but they give you the most efficient way to get to the next step. Feel free to adapt this script, however, I've found it works really well, so to start, you can just copy it!

Before I show it to you, there are some really key points you want to include in your outreach email.

Key Points To include:

- demand potential;
- exact specifications;
- complete bundle required;
- number of units;
- delivery terms;
- delivery address;

SUPPLIER OUTREACH SCRIPT

Hi There,

My Name is **[NAME]** from **[COMPANY]**. I am looking to purchase **[PRODUCT]** for the **[UK]** market.

My primary sales channel will be online through [] and estimate up to **[10,000–15,000]** pieces sold annually after I have a trial order of **[200]** units to sample and evaluate.

Specifications Required:

- [PRODUCT]
- [Size]
- [Material]
- [Colour]
- Custom Logo **[printed/sewn/etched (insert relevant method)]**
- Custom Packaging

I've seen you manufacture these items. Can you please provide me with the following:

- Quotation for the above specifications for Air Express Door to Door (Ideally DDP or DAP) shipping to the follow address (Use *The following address is just for shipping estimate*):
    - Unit 1,
    - Kingston Park,
    - Flaxley Road,
    - Peterborough
    - PE2 9EN
    - United Kingdom
- Can you confirm if you are the Manufacturer or a Trading Company?
- What is the rough cost for a sample with shipping by air express to the UK?
- We are looking to bundle this product with [example]. Do you manufacture this also?
- How many units do you pack per carton?

Thank you for your time,

Kind Regards

[NAME] [COMPANY]

Once you've adapted this script for your product, then you can start sending it to suppliers.

When starting your supplier outreach, it's just a numbers game. If you reach out to just three suppliers, then you're going to find it hard to really assess the true cost and get a good deal. Many suppliers will not reply, however using this script, I've found it to be the most effective as it commands authority.

When searching on *alibaba.com*, I would send this message to around twenty suppliers, then take notice of who came back quickly, and who took a little longer. This can be a sign of how busy they are. A busier supplier is less likely to give you such a good price as they don't need your business as much.

Lastly, when reaching out to suppliers, be aware of the time difference. If you're in the UK like me, then early morning is best for sending and replying to emails. Often, I will speak to my suppliers first thing when I wake up as you'll get quick responses. If you leave your replies until late in the day, you'll most likely be waiting until the next day for a reply. If you want to get the quickest results, I would always dedicate some time in the morning for this rather than in the evening.

STEP #2: FOCUS ON THE SUPPLIER WITH THE BEST PRICE VS QUALITY

Very often, people can be hypnotised by a low price from a supplier but later find out after they've ordered a sample that the quality is awful, and they've wasted their time and money just because they saw a low price. It's important to not be deluded by low prices as this normally equals poor quality products, and then by extension, you won't be able to sell to your customers for as much.

Once you know that you're dealing with a supplier that

has a good quality product, then make the first offer. This is called 'Setting an Anchor' (a starting point). Remember, never give your price ceiling, but give them an offer that is intentionally low that doesn't insult them by being ridiculous. As you've now had prices from multiple suppliers, you'll understand more about the true cost, so if the true cost is around $4 then don't go offering $1. They will just ignore your offer and think that you're taking the piss.

If they make the first offer, then be sure to 're-anchor' the price. For example, they say, 'The lowest we can do is $3 per unit'. You would come back and re-anchor the price, and say something like, 'Okay, thank you for that. The highest I can go at the moment is $2.45. Can you get any closer to this? Maybe if you can ask your boss in this case?'

It's important to always be respectful, and even though I said that $2.45 was the highest I can go, of course, it's not, as you never give your price ceiling.

STEP 3: EXPAND THE NEGOTIATION

At this point, you can expand the negotiation. Let's say the price point has no wiggle room, and they are not willing to negotiate any further. This doesn't mean negotiations are over. It means you need to expand the scope of the negotiations.

Two examples of this may be to reduce the minimum order quantity (MOQ) by actually increasing the price. For example, you could say, the only way I could go as high as $3 per unit is if I reduced the MOQ to 250. On the other hand, you may be able to reduce the cost by increasing MOQ. For example, if you asked, 'Can you do $2.45 per unit if I increase the MOQ to 1,000?'

Don't be put off by this. You might not order 1,000 units on your first order, however it gives you scope on what they can negotiate to. This gives you wiggle room. Once they've given the price for 1,000 units, then you can negotiate to 500 units and meet in the middle for the unit cost.

Another example may be bundled products, product inserts, packaging and even the number of colours on your packaging. These are all costs that add up and if you can save just $0.10 per unit on the packaging, it's worth doing.

With negotiating, there is a certain level of bullshitting so you can get as much info from them as possible. It's also important to keep some cards close to your chest. Just remember that they aren't experts in negotiation, so, by using these strategies, you can often get a much better deal, and a better deal means more profit for you!

ENSURING YOU ALWAYS GET THE BEST QUALITY

We've covered quality quite a bit, so this section will be pretty swift but must be noted, nevertheless.

"Let me ask you, when was the last time you left a review on *Amazon*?

For most of you, it would be 'never', and for some of you, it would be few and far between. However, I can bet that the people who have, probably left a negative review, right?" As humans, we focus so much on the negative and getting a one-star review is easier than you might think. Just one slip-up can lead to a brutal review, so you want to protect against this at all costs.

If you have twenty reviews when you start, and you get just two bad reviews, that's 10% of all reviews, which has a drastic impact. Fortunately, most of the time, these can be averted. The number one reason why you'll get bad reviews is a faulty product, so what's the best way to prevent against these reviews? A GOOD PRODUCT! It's as simple as that, do as much as you can to test your products, and really stress-test them as a customer would. If you find a design flaw in the product, then you can address it.

What you don't want to do is not test the product, then the first time you get feedback is from angry customers. This can kill the business. However, if the product is tested correctly, it can give your businesses everlasting success!

CALCULATING YOUR PROFIT MARGINS SO THERE'S NO HIDDEN SURPRISES

The amount of times that I've seen people completely ignore costs is outstanding, and the reason why is mostly because they are what I call 'unconsciously ignorant'. This means you don't know what you don't know. This is why it's so important to learn from someone who has done it before and learn the process in one go rather than going to three different people as you may lose key information in the process.

There are so many variables to consider with costs, as such that's why I give my SellerPro Academy students access to my profit calculator. But for now, here's how you can start to figure it out.

There are two costs you will look at:

- Landed Cost (to *Amazon*);
- Landed Cost (to Customer).

These are the two costs you'll really need to know which are essentially, how much does it cost to get your product to *Amazon*'s warehouse (or anywhere else), and how much does it cost you to sell the product and get it to the customer? If you work these out incorrectly, it can cause disasters with your finances. so, listen up.

LANDED COST (TO AMAZON)

The 'Landed Cost to *Amazon*' is the total cost of a product/shipment once it has arrived at the *Amazon* Fulfilment Centre.

This will include:

- product cost (physical and digital);
- shipping costs (including insurance);
- customs duties;
- VAT;
- currency conversion/payment fees.

LANDED COST (TO CUSTOMER)

The 'Landed Cost to Customer' is the total cost of your product to get it into a customer's hand.

This will include:

- Landed Cost to *Amazon*;
- *Amazon* selling fee;
- FBA fee;
- *Amazon* membership (monthly);
- advertising.

You will also have secondary business costs that may not have a direct impact per unit, but you may use them to run your business or set up the product, such as:

- email marketing service;
- marketing materials (graphic design);

- bookkeeper;

- accountant;

- outsourcers.

After all of this, of course, you'll have the dreaded tax bill. So, always be sure to account for VAT in your costs, and once you're registered for VAT, account for it in your sales price. I would always advise seeking professional advice from a licensed accountant.

No one likes doing the maths, but you know what everyone hates? Losing money!

Make sure you take this time to get it right and remember that every percent you save on your product costs is an extra percent you make in profit!

07
UNIQUE SELLING POINTS (USPs) DON'T EXIST.

For the better part of my life I've always been taught that the only way to stand out is to have a unique selling point (USP). As a teenager I grew up watching Dragons Den on TV where entrepreneurs pitch their business idea to a panel of successful business owners known as 'The Dragons' then after a Q&A they have the option to invest.

Time after time entrepreneurs would pitch to the dragons and often the push back would be that their business has no USP so they are un-able to invest.

This is what I believed and possibly what you believe right now.

But let me tell you, USPs don't exist.

Of course, at one point they did however the features that make those products unique are soon copied. Then because of all the new competition, companies innovate and add extra features or selling points, which subsequently get copied. This means that nothing is really unique, as it can be easily copied.

Think about the iPhone when it first came out. They had a unique selling point, a device that had a full size touch screen, could make calls, access the internet and have your music library all in one. At the time it was revolutionary and they truly had a unique selling point. It wasn't long before other companies copied them and released their own versions at which point; the features are no longer unique. This cycle of innovation and imitation is still going on to this day and will continue on for a long time yet.

So, what happens when the USP doesn't exist?

Let's say you want to go and buy a new car and you have narrowed down your choice to a BMW, Audi or a Mercedes.

You can compare statistics and consume hours' worth of reviews, but at their core all three create similar cars. The way you perceive them is very different.

Rather than each having a USP, they instead have an Owned Emotional Selling Point (OESP).

BMW - *"The Ultimate Driving Machine"*

Audi - *"Vorsprung Durch Technik"* Translated to *"Being Ahead through Technology"*

Mercedes - *"The Best or Nothing"*

For years these companies have marketed themselves to align with these statements that they own.

For BMW you automatically think that they are a driver's car, they are more thrilling, more raw and perfect for someone that thoroughly enjoys the drive.

Equally with Audi, they want customers that love a more technical car (even though they may be no more technical then their other German competitors).

With Mercedes they have made themselves into a brand of luxury and target consumers that want only the best when in reality, they use materials no different to that of Audi and BMW.

These are their owned emotional selling points they focus on a customer avatar and target a customer that wants to feel the real driving experience, or someone that wants to feel like they have the best technology at their fingertips or someone who wants to live in luxury and feel important.

They all focus on the emotions of their ideal customer and how the product will make them feel rather than what it will actually do for them.

Can you think about what makes Nike's trainers so innovative?

Thought not, however what's the one phrase you think about immediately when you think of Nike?

"Just Do It"

This isn't a feature, but an owned emotional selling point. It speaks to their core mission and evokes emotion in its customers and gives Nike a greater purpose than just selling footwear.

You may be thinking, 'that's great Jonny, but how does that help me?"

What you now need to do is attach an owned emotional selling point to your brand.

When I created one of my brands; HydroFuel, I did exactly that and came up with the tagline and OESP, "Fuel Your Future."

As my goal is to change the hydration habits of my customers what I really wanted to do is give my customers the chance to fuel themselves correctly through proper hydration. The features you have and the products you sell will change, but the message will stay consistent.

When I asked a friend about what they think about when I say, "HydroFuel." They immediately replied not with the features of the product but with, "fuel your future." So, I asked what that statement meant to them and they told me that it was all about giving your body what it needs to perform, whether that's mentally or physically.

This tagline could have easily been left off. Something

as simple as a tagline can evoke the emotional attachment to your brand that allows you to not only make the sale but keep the customer for longer as they can relate to your mission.

For a while I was just, 'the amazon guy' with no real OESP. My training was built around being the best and having the most advanced lessons and support however something was missing; I was missing an OESP.

I started introducing the following statement; *"Remember, you're just one product away..."*

For me this means that all it takes is one success to completely change your life. I've seen this with myself and with countless students I've mentored. The point of the sentence being unfinished as it allows you to fill in the gap with the outcome you're looking for. Success is subjective, so who am I to tell you what success should look like for you.

Your aim is to create a brand and a product that when customers buy it, they start to love it. They go home after work and over dinner talk about the cool new product they bought. When a friend asks them for a recommendation, they automatically think of you, maybe not because you even have the best and most advanced product in the market, but because you have the brand that connected with them emotionally.

There are two keys to creating an owned emotional selling point:

- Make it about a cause greater than just the brand;

- OWN the statement.

This means that firstly, your OESP is not about the product directly, for example, "We have the best material," wouldn't work as it is about the product and has no greater meaning. Your OESP should be relatable to your target audience and form a thought in their head that is more than just about a product or brand. It must connect with their desires about where they want to be or about who they are today.

Secondly, once you create this statement, you must OWN it. This means that you're proud to put your tag line on your packaging, website, marketing and even your product.

Use your OESP to communicate who you are to your customers.

You've just learned about how your brand should showcase how it makes customers feel rather than what the products do for them. Equally a brand name is just as influential.

CREATING A BRAND NAME THAT STANDS OUT FROM THE CROWD

Before I knew about what made a good brand name, I would base my decisions purely on if I liked the name, if it *sounded* good or from my gut feeling. Most business owners do this, as when you're thinking about creating a name that represents your brand you always think about how it makes *you* feel rather than how you think it'll make the customer feel.

Once you shift perspective and look at your brand name from the customers point of view, you'll be able to align with their thoughts and feelings to create a brand that your customers can relate to, rather than a brand that *you* relate to.

You might also think that you want to get the *perfect* brand name, one that just rolls off the tongue and represents everything you stand for. Unfortunately, this rarely exists. Often the *perfect* name is already taken.

You need to name your brand for the customer, not you.

Three things you need before creating your name:

- analyse your competition;
- know your vision;
- understand your brand personality.

ANALYSE YOUR COMPETITION

Before you name your brand it's important that you first analyse your competition. You do this so you can make sure that you can stand out. If the majority have logos that are green and start with 'The' then make sure your brand isn't green and doesn't start with 'The.'

To be memorable you need to stand out and offer the customer a new opportunity rather than an improvement.

KNOW YOUR VISION

It's easy to say that you stand for 'quality' or ' integrity,' the issue is that these are generic. Instead finish this sentence:

We are here to create a world in which...

For example, my education business' vision is to create a world in which ordinary people can create extraordinary things, so I can change people's lives one product at a time.

The statement you create is for your internal use only and it's not a statement that will go on your website or your packaging. It is something that you use as a filter when making decisions. So, before you decide on your brand name, understand what it is that you stand for.

UNDERSTAND YOUR BRAND PERSONALITY

Each brand has a place in its market, so you need to decide what kind of brand you'll be. This could be fun, practical, cost effective, luxury, sporty, modern and so on.

You wouldn't see *Gucci* release a low end, low quality product as it doesn't align with their luxury fashion brand. H&M on the other hand would be comfortable releasing lower quality, less luxurious clothing as they are a mainstream lower end fashion brand. Equally you wouldn't see H&M start selling fishing gear as they are not an outdoor sports market.

Spend time coming up with as many names as you can and don't worry about coming up with names that are bad. It's all part of the process to get your ideas flowing.

Once you've come up with a big list, it's time to create a shortlist.

CREATING YOUR SHORTLIST

It's important to mention that you will not be able to reflect everything that you want to in your brand name, it's just not possible. If your brand is a luxury one you may not have a luxury sounding name, for example *Gucci* is a luxury brand, but the word *Gucci* heard alone sounds more like you're speaking to a baby than about a high-end clothing brand. On the flipside, their visual brand does reflect their luxury nature in a more compelling way.

Generally, names need to be easy to spell, easily spoken and short. There's nothing more frustrating when you're looking for a brand that you've heard about from a friend and you can't spell their name or even remember the entire name as it was too long. For big brands it's sometimes okay as they may have put millions into brand awareness. For startups, you want to make it easy for the customer to know who you are so they can find you.

Your brand name has two influential moments:

- The first time it's seen/heard;
- The second time it's seen/heard.

The first time you see/hear a brand name it needs to be unique, capture attention and show you what the brand is all about.

The second time you see a brand name it must reinforce everything you've learned about it previously as a brand name represents who you are to your customers.

A brand name is the only part of your brand that can go anywhere; print, audio, video etc. so make sure that the word(s) are a clear representation of who you are as a company.

Once you have a short list of names conduct legal due diligence checks to make sure that they will most likely be available. Quick searches can bring up conflicts with:

- existing registered company names;
- registered trademarks;
- domain names;
- social handles.

At this point you will also want to make sure potential names are not solely available in your country but in any you wish to service. If any of those countries have a language different to yours then conduct a check to make sure your names do not translate into anything offensive.

You can conduct in-depth searches or hire a lawyer to research the availability of these names in detail however only do that once you have chosen a name as conducting searches on five names will of course cost five times as much as just one. If it turns out that there's a conflict, then just go back to your shortlist to pick another.

After you've got your OESP and brand name decided you'll be armed with everything you need to start dominating your market. All the preparation and work you've done to create the product and brand have been approached from the customers perspective; this is why you'll dominate.

In the next chapter you're going learn about how to create a high converting listing. Similar to the previous sections, you're going to approach it from the customers perspective.

If there's just one lesson you pick up from this book, let it be that you need to have genuine empathy for your customers and to truly put them first at every turn.

Unique Selling Points (usps) Don't Exist.

08
CREATING THE PERFECT LISTING

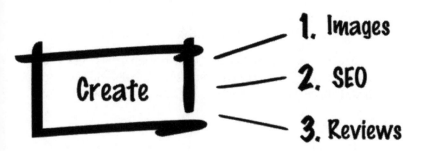

I recently read a book called, "Insanely Simple" by Ken Segall. Segall worked on the 'think different' advertising Campaign for Apple and he was the person who named the iMac.

He shares a story about a meeting he had with Steve Jobs and their ad agency about a new ad campaign they were working on for the debut for the first iMac.

Steve wanted to show the top 5 features of the iMac in the 30 second ad slot as he believed they were all really important points that the customer should know. However, Lee Chow one of the leaders at the ad agency; Chiat/Day was insisting that the entire spot was dedicated to just one feature that they believed to be the most important.

After some debate Lee abruptly ripped off 5 pages from his note pad and scrunched them up into balls. He took one ball and threw it at Steve who caught it and threw it back.

"That's a good ad," said Lee

He then threw all 5 balls at Steve; he didn't catch a single one.

"That's a bad ad," said Lee

I loved this story as it shows that the more things you ask someone to focus on the fewer they'll be able to remember.

It's just like when you're creating your images for your

Amazon listing as these are essentially, advertisements. Not only do you have to make sure the customer can catch the ball but you also have to be able to cater to the tiny attention span of customers as they navigate online.

To explain to you just how short peoples' attention spans are and how quickly they make decisions based on looks and looks alone, let me tell you a quick story.

I was at a mate's house just the other day. He had just split up with his girlfriend and thought it was time to get back in the game, so he downloaded a popular dating app for the first time.

I hadn't used this app before, it didn't exist the last time I was single, but it was fascinating for me to watch him swipe mostly left within split seconds of seeing these girls' pictures. I mean, it was probably three swipes per second. So, within a third of a second, he has made a decision about whether this person is worth a cheeky swipe right. Our ability to make decisions within split seconds is astounding.

Another great example is when my girlfriend scrolls through Netflix just looking at the cover images and not actually checking the title to see what the film is actually about. We all do this. You make decisions every day based on looks alone, so why would you expect the shoppers on *Amazon* be any different?

The 3 steps to creating a killer product listing

- functional design formula;

- search engine optimisation (SEO);

- reviews.

Look at the two images below, which one are your eyes are drawn to most?

I now want you to think about why your eyes are drawn to the one on the right.

Think about what part of the photo you're looking at. For example, are you looking at the phone screen, the box, the bottle or the blue disk ... or are you looking at all four? My point is that the photo on the right is significantly more interesting than the one on the left. So, when a customer has these two options in front of them, which one do you think they are going to choose?

You have to understand that 90% of the reason why a customer will click on your product is because of the way it looks. We are shallow beings and are driven mostly by what we see, and this is where you can absolutely dominate the market.

Before I move on to talk about the three areas that create a killer product listing, I want to show you another image.

And finally, you will read this.

YOU WILL READ THIS FIRST.

And then you will read this.
Followed closely by this.

I am showing you this to explain that the human brain is predictable, you can communicate in very specific ways when you know how the human brain operates. Although you aren't going to be so obvious on your images, notice how the thing you read first is the biggest and it's highlighted with the black stripe. You then move to the next biggest line of text and then as you read left to right and up to down, you see the bottom line, then suddenly realise there was one more part to the photo and look up.

Remember, your brain is predictable. To create images in this way, you use a method called 'the functional design formula'.

THE FUNCTIONAL DESIGN FORMULA

Your images are about 90% of the reason why a customer will click on your product and buy it, yet many sellers neglect this completely by uploading complicated, confusing, and poorly designed images. As we've discussed, people make decisions based on what looks good extremely quickly, so when done correctly, you can really stand out from the competition. However, when done badly, you'll struggle to make sales, and ultimately, you'll be leaving thousands of pounds on the table for your competitors to pick up.

For a long time, I would struggle to communicate functional design fully to my mentees, it was something I knew for myself but couldn't articulate. One day I went to tackle this issue head on and I locked myself in my office, got the Flipchart out and wrote on the board, "The Functional Design Formula" For the next two hours I wrote down idea after idea, just like how I've taught you to do so. After getting fed up, I called up a friend and colleague William Richards, owner of In A Nutshell Creative. William is responsible for every image, logo, design element that I use in my business, he knows my preferences inside out and understands exactly how I operate when it comes to communicating through design.

I shared my progress and told him that I wanted a three-step formula to creating insanely high converting images for your Amazon listing. I asked him to think back to all the times he had worked on his own images and to think about what are the three influential things that when put together can be used as a weapon to convert customers to buy.

He then said something that changed everything.

He told me, "Well, it's really all about clarity isn't it?"

At that point I had immense clarity and yet another Vu Jádé.

I scribbled on the Flipchart these 3 words:

- communicate

- clarity

- consistency

After I wrote these down, my brain had a burst of ideas as everything fell into place. I told William that I'd call him back later as I need to get all these ideas onto paper before I forget them.

Here's how it works.

Firstly, you have to understand two misconceptions that are common when people design their images:

- "If the images look good, then a customer will buy it."

- " If the image has loads of information on it, it is more valuable."

Before you move on understand that a 'pretty' image doesn't mean it is high converting. Some of the best images can be 'ugly' however they convert at higher rates. Also understand that each image has a very specific purpose and too much information leads to indecision from the customer.

COMMUNICATE

Ask yourself :

- what am I trying to communicate to the customer?

- why am I communicating it?

- does it help the customer?

Write down the answers now.

WHAT AM I TRYING TO COMMUNICATE TO THE CUSTOMER?

_____

_____

_____

_____

_____

_____

WHY AM I COMMUNICATING IT?

_____

_____

_____

_____

_____

_____

DOES IT HELP THE CUSTOMER?

_____

_____

_____

_____

_____

_____

Having done this you'd now have a clear idea of what you want to communicate and why it's important for the customer. This step is influential as once you know what your customers want, you can truly communicate with them on a higher level.

Your next step is to write down a list of the top 3-5 features of your product in order of importance (Make sure the biggest feature that differentiates you from the competition it high up on the list).

LIST OF FEATURES

_____

_____

_____

_____

_____

_____

Now allocate a feature to each one of the 5 photo spots you have available on Amazon (Leave the 1st for your Hero image and the 7th for a lifestyle image, this leaves you with 5 images out of the 7 available).

WHAT DO I INCLUDE IN EACH IMAGE?

Many sellers get this so wrong, and they try to jam as much information into one image as possible as they think that the more information that they give the customer, the better the image will be. However, this couldn't be farther from the truth. On any one picture, you should only be trying to communicate one feature – two at the most.

If you have four main features of the product, then split those up into four images. This way, the customer flicks through them at about one image per half a second, then they know exactly what the product is and what it does as the images have communicated just one feature at a time making it super easy for the brain to pick it up.

I have a great test for this.

Once you've had your images designed, bring them up on your phone (always use a phone as most shoppers use mobiles now), then give your phone to a friend who doesn't know much about the product. Ask them to scroll through as they would if they were shopping. After they've scrolled through ask them these questions:

- what is the product?

- what does it come with?

- what stood out to you?

If the answers you get are not what you were trying to communicate, then you've got it wrong. You didn't create images that clearly communicated what you were trying to say. So, you go back to the drawing board, you make amendments, and you do the process again with someone else.

This is also important for the order of the images.

IMAGE ORDER

When I was doing this process, I showed my images to a few friends, but none of them were saying that one of the main features was that the HydroFuel Bottle comes with an app. I was shocked as there's a whole image dedicated to it. The issue wasn't the image, it was the order as I had that image last. Most people stop paying attention, or don't make it to the last image, so never know that it's included. I made one simple change and moved it from last to second, just after the main image. I conducted the same experiment with different people, and all of a sudden, they started saying that the bottle came with an app.

The smallest changes can have the biggest results, but you have to do these experiments first. You have to test your images and think about it always from the customers' point of view. I've been through many of my students' images before and just simply changing the order to align with the most important features and splitting up some images that had too much information can have meaningful impacts. Some peoples' business went from making two to three sales a day to over 30! All from some subtle changes to their images.

CLARITY

It's great that you now have a really strong idea about what you're communicating to your customer and in what order however if the customer doesn't have clarity then the features will be lost and you'll potentially lose the sale.

The main questions we'll be answering is this:

- how do I communicate my features at a glance?
- how do I make sure that the customer will understand?

This is broken down into 4 areas:

- what images to use
- the image layout
- the text layout and font size
- annotations and graphics

WHAT IMAGES TO USE

As you only have a handful of photos to 'wow' the customer you need to make sure they are used to the best of their ability. One way to do this is by not repeating images. Quite often I'll see sellers that use the same product image multiple times over a few photos. They think that they need to show the main product photo in each image so that the customer knows how good it is. However, as soon as you use an image more than once it becomes a waste of space.

You need to use the real estate that you have in a smart way, and duplicating images and having small changes or additional features highlighted will not communicate the features in the best way. Be sure that you don't use the same product photo twice.

Instead if you're wishing to showcase a feature of the product do not use the picture you've used previously but use a product photo that showcases that feature. This could be up close or from a different angle.

Finally, use high quality product photography or 3D renders so that your product images look high end. By having high quality images, you build trust with your customers and subconsciously it shows them that you're a trusted brand. Later on in this chapter I'll tell you how to get high end product photography arranged at a low cost.

IMAGE LAYOUT

Personally, I use a theoretical template when creating images, here it is.

Image 1 (Hero):

Shows the main product and everything that comes with it in one image. Make sure it looks lifelike in terms of sizes of the different bundled items – just as if you had laid everything out on a table, everything is in proportion. Where possible, use 3D renders if the product is suitable for this. Make sure the product fills up around 80% of the white area and put the product on a white background. This image is most important as it's the first image a customer sees in their search results. Take screenshots of all of your competitors' images and then make sure yours stands out from the crowd so that customers' eyes are drawn to it.

Once you capture their attention, you're one step closer to capturing a sale.

To test your image, search for the product using the main keyword, and take a screenshot of that page. Then edit that screenshot and put your image as one of the search results. Send this to a few friends and ask them which one they would click on. Tally up the results, and if yours isn't getting the most 'clicks', then get back to the drawing board again, make some changes, and repeat the experiment again until your image is the clear winner.

You may be reading this thinking that you don't need to do that to know what looks good and while I appreciate the ego... lose it. It doesn't matter what you think about the image; it only matters what customers think. Remember that they are making subconscious decisions so when you analyse the image with your conscious brain, you actually have no idea what customers are seeing.

If you want to have success, more success, than all of your competition, then you need to be conducting these experiments until you've nailed it.

Trust me, you'll thank me later!

Images 2–6:

This is where you split up your most important features, going from the most important to the least.

You also need to think about what differentiates your products compared to your competition as you need customers to know what makes you different as soon as possible. So, your defining, unique feature should be the second or third photo but no later. The way I like the think about it is, if you were telling someone about your product in person, what would you say and in what order? Then you have to make sure your images reflect that.

Again, conduct experiments with this until it's right.

Image 7+

On *Amazon*, you have the ability (at the time of writing) to add up to nine images, however only seven are viewable on mobile, and as most shop on mobile, I would focus on seven. This is where you can add lifestyle photos. These are just photos of the product being used in real life. Do not use 3D renders or photoshop to superimpose your product onto a random image. Customers can tell that you've faked it, and you'll lose your customers' trust. For these images, they must always be high quality, and they must clearly show the product in use. The reason you do this is so the customer can imagine what it would be like if they had the product. It also will give the customer a better idea of the size, colour, material etc.

Text layout and font size

At a glance your customers need to know what each image is communicating, an efficient way to do this is use titles on each image. To come up with the title think of the simplest way to communicate the feature then if your title is more than three words see if there are any words you can cut out. This is because at a glance you can read three words in a microsecond. Any more than five words then it becomes a sentence that you have to read.

If you have bullet points or annotations keep this to no more than three at a time and again keep the word count to a minimum. If you can say it in less words, say it in less words.

For headings use larger or bold fonts and for keywords make them bold to stand out. The reason you may want to make keywords bold is because the readers eye will **naturally be drawn** to them. If those keywords **communicate** the feature then this will help the customer take in everything you're communicating at a **glance** as by showing them what's the most **important,** you've helped them take it in quicker.

Finally, do not use hard to read fonts. You need to make reading the text on your images as simple as possible.

Annotations and graphics

Annotations and graphics are used to help customers join the dots. So, if there is a particular feature you want to pull focus to you can use a line or subtle graphic to pull the focus of the customers eye to it.

Make sure that any annotations or graphics you use do not pull focus from the product or main point of the image. This means nothing over the top, in your face or so big and bright that you can't help but look at it. The perfect use of graphics is when you don't even notice they're there.

CONSISTENCY

You may think that consistency is all about doing the same thing again and again but actually for me consistency is about how you become familiar in micro-seconds, or how you create predictability with your design. For me, consistency does not mean, 'the same.'

Break this down into five areas:

- brand consistency
- colour consistency
- graphic consistency

- layout consistency

- voice consistency

Brand consistency

Your brand is not what you tell yourself, it's what your customers tell you. This means that you can say you have a 'luxury' brand, however if your customers don't see that then you don't have a luxury brand.

When creating your images make sure that they all reflect what you want your brand to represent. This may be simplicity, luxury, convenience or enjoyment. Take influence from similar companies that have a brand image similar to what you'd like.

Colour Consistency

Pick your brand colours and stick to them. Try to stick to 3 main colours (excluding Black and white).

Think about your brand image and use the colours that best represents it. For example, a 'old fashioned' brand image wouldn't have super bright vibrant colours as they would be out of place.

Your brain is wired to see contrast and things that stick out so create contrast with your colours, use this to your advantage to highlight features or things you want your customers to pay attention to.

Graphic consistency

Remember that graphics and annotations are there to help the customer join the dots, use them to direct the customer to what you want them to see. Keep it simple as it's easy to over complicate, do this by using the least amount of graphics as possible yet still be effective. Finally, align the colours to make sure that the graphics align with your brand image.

Layout consistency

We've discussed layout in theory however before you get your images made then I would recommend you create an actual template for a designer to take influence from. Remember that people (in the west) read from left to right, top to bottom. Create a layout guide which shows where roughly you want the product, the title, annotations and text. It doesn't t have to be beautiful, it is there just to help the designer understand how you want.

Voice consistency

A brand voice is how you communicate through the choice of words. Your voice shows the reader or listener the attitude, values and personality of the brand. Think about how your brand speaks so to align with its identity. For example, you wouldn't want to use a scientific voice for a brand this is meant to be friendly and fun. When creating any copy think about what words you use for example:

- be casual but not lazy

- professional but not bossy

- clinical but not confusing

- fun but not inappropriate

- conversational but not sloppy

- authoritative but not too serious

- confident but not cocky

So that you always align with your brand voice create a simple brief where you can put all the do's and do not's. For example:

Voice Characteristic: Authoritative

Description: Your content should be well researched and sound confident in its accuracy.

Do: Create detailed copy that reassures the reader that you're an expert

Do not: Sound too friendly, clinical or confusing

Voice Characteristic: Funny

Description: Our content is okay with making people laugh.

Do: Use humour with care

Do not: Be too weird or inappropriate

VOICE CHARACTERISTIC:

_____

_____

_____

_____

_____

_____

DESCRIPTION:

_____

_____

_____

_____

_____

_____

DO:

_____

_____

_____

_____

_____

_____

DON'T:

_____

_____

_____

_____

_____

_____

We've now covered the three steps to the functional design formula; Communicate, Clarity, Consistency. As promised here is a sneaky trick on how you can get high quality images taken of your product without paying high prices.

GETTING HIGH QUALITY PHOTOS AT A LOW COST

It doesn't have to be expensive to have photos taken, sometimes you can do them yourself, but here's an awesome trick to get photographers and models super cheap. One way you can get photographers and models is to *Google* to find companies that do this; however, they often charge ten times what you actually can get these done for. The way I do it is far cheaper, it'll take a little legwork, but in the long term it's preferred.

Here's how you do it:

Step 1: Go onto *Facebook* and search in groups for 'Photographers [Insert your location]'. For example, if you lived in Cambridge, you would search for, 'Photographers Cambridge', and join those groups.

Do the same for 'Models [location]'.

Step 2: After you've joined the groups, create a post like this:

'Hey everyone, I have a small company selling [PRODUCT] and looking for a [photographer/model] on [DATE] in [LOCATION]. I have a small budget and will need you for [HOURS]. The shoot will be demonstrating the product [go on to say what sort of images you want].

Please, can you comment with the link to your portfolio if you're interested and can make this date, time and location.

I will PM you if I am interested.

Thank you!'

Step 3: Go through the responses, check their portfolios, and message the people who you think will be good.

Step 4: Ask for their hourly rate, and if it's too high for you, say 'thank you' and explain what your budget is. Say if they are happy to do it for that, then perfect, but if not, then thank them for their time and move on to someone who will do it. This may take some time just talking to people on *Facebook*, but you will find people who are good and willing to do it within your price range.

For example, for the HydroFuel photoshoots, I hired about eight models paying between £20 and £35 per hour depending on their portfolio. Now, you wouldn't need eight models, however, I went a little overboard as I was creating content for social media adverts rather than just a couple of images to go on *Amazon*.

I could have done this with one model and just one hour of time, costing maybe £30 for the model and maybe £30–50 for a photographer. In fact, when I released a new colour, I just used my iPhone and me as the model. You can be thrifty, but make sure you value quality over everything. Do not upload low-quality images onto your listing, ever. If you need studio space, you can again go into these same groups and put a post out looking for studio space. Many people will have spaces that you can use at a fraction of the cost compared to if you just used *Google* and searched.

SEO – SEARCH ENGINE OPTIMISATION

The first real step to this is understanding what keywords are the most powerful for you. I guess even before that, you need to know... 'What is a keyword, anyway'?

A keyword is simply a word or phrase a customer would type into the search bar to find your product.

As an example, if you wanted headphones you might search for:

- headphones;
- Bluetooth headphones
- wireless headphones;
- over-ear headphones;
- over-ear wireless headphones;
- and so on...

Let me ask you some questions.

How does *Amazon* know to show your product to customers when they search for it? Are there employees sitting there manually doing this? Of course not. The key to understanding the *Amazon* algorithm is to understand two fundamental facts:

- *Amazon's* goal is to provide the best service and

products to their customers.

- *Amazon* is actually just a search engine for products.

When you search for a product, *Amazon* wants to show you the most relevant products and ones that have the best feedback, the most popular, and best value for money. That is how they serve their customers, by providing them with an exceptional service. To do this, they rank each product based on numerous metrics. As a seller, you want to give *Amazon* the best information about your product so their algorithm understands exactly what your product is and can display it to the relevant customers. That is why SEO is so important. It is the optimisation of your product listing so it can be found via searching.

There are two places where *Amazon* take the bulk of their data from your listing.

- your title;

- your search term keywords.

Have you ever been looking at Amazon and seen a title like this?

Wireless Headphones Bluetooth, Up to 9 Hrs Playing Time Mpow IPX7 Waterproof Running Headphones In-ear Earbuds for Gym Cycling Workout iPhone,iPad,Samsung, Siri with Built-in Noise Cancelling Mic
★★★★★ ˅ 3,548
£18²⁹ £22.99
✓prime Get it by Tomorrow, May 30

Did you ever think, why can't they just have the title as 'Bluetooth Headphones'?

The reason why all good sellers have titles like this is that Amazon looks at your title for an indication about what your product is.

For example, if you're selling wireless headphones, you probably won't find 'Pokémon Cards' in the title.

SEO isn't something just for selling on Amazon. If you have a website, a blog, a *YouTube* video, or basically anything else that is searchable online, you'll want to know what SEO is and how you can use it to your advantage.

Secondly, there is an investible area within Amazon where sellers can put their most powerful keywords. This isn't visible to the customers, but it is visible to Amazon. The keywords you enter work in exactly the same way as your title, so if you get these wrong or simply don't fill them out, you're leaving thousands on the table.

In essence, the greater number of keywords you rank for, the more searches you show up for. The more searches you show up for and the higher you rank for those keywords, the more money you make.

We can use keyword tools freely available on the Internet for ideas on what customers are searching for, however, if you want the exact numbers, you can use paid services like keywordtool.io or helium10.com. Both of these offer keyword finding tools where you type in a keyword, like 'headphones', and it will show you all the ones related to it and even show you how many people are searching each month!

Once armed with this data, you can go on to create a listing that is jam-packed full of the juiciest keywords so now Amazon will know exactly who to show your product to when they search.

HOW TO GET REVIEWS ON AUTOPILOT

Reviews are the lifeblood of any business, and that's never been truer than on websites like Amazon. There are a few areas that pretty much every customer looks at when searching for a product to buy:

- pictures;
- price;
- reviews.

If you have wicked images, a price that shows great value for money, but bad or no reviews, then your business is doomed. Even if you have hundreds of amazing reviews, customers will always want to see the 1-Star reviews, so they know what happens when you get it wrong or when a customer feels like you've done wrong by them.

We are going to discuss how to ethically get reviews for your product and how to handle complaints when they eventually do come in. This means that you're going to be getting tonnes of positive and real reviews, and you'll also have great responses and approach to customer service when things aren't going as well.

HOW TO GET REVIEWS ON AUTOPILOT

Unfortunately, there are many people out there that are happy to wear a black hat (a hat worn by those who are bad) when it comes to getting reviews, and you will see this happen in nearly every business where reviews are public facing. Amazon and other sites are cracking down on fake reviews, so this is how you ensure that you are not affected negatively by this. In fact, if you approach getting reviews in the way I'm about to show you, any efforts Amazon take to remove fake reviews will only help you and hurt your competition!

DON'T SELL BAD PRODUCTS

We've discussed quality earlier in the book, but this is so

important with getting positive reviews. Even the smallest issue can take a 5-Star down to a 1-Star.

Have you ever been to a restaurant where the food was incredible, the service was quick, the bill was reasonable, but there was draft coming in from an open door that ruined your whole experience because you were cold? Of course, you may not have had this exact experience, but you get my point, right? Even if the product is perfect, just one thing can turn a promotor into a detractor. This can be something as simple as the corner of the package was bent, or it arrived two hours late.

Fortunately, if you're selling on Amazon and you get any issues like that, Amazon takes the blame for it, removes the review, and if the customer is refunded, Amazon will reimburse you for the product that they damaged. However, what happens if the product had a scratch, or worse, there was a fundamental quality issue with the product where one out of every 10 customers had an issue?

The first step is having a great product that's high quality that customers will love.

This may not be true, but I was told that Apple has a team of people that are just there to test the 'unboxing experience' of their products. Think about it; they want the first experience with their new product to be as happy as possible. However, a lot of the stuff you order online comes in a jiffy bag in a brown box with no packaging which doesn't lead to an incredibly fulfilling unboxing experience.

Something you can do very easily is to have custom packaging that is designed to a high standard so that when a customer receives your product, they are happy straight away, even if there were a few hiccups. What you'll find is that people can tell when care has gone into the design of a product and it's packaging, and their response and attitude towards you will change. They will respect you more as a company. If your product arrives with no box, no branding, and is broken, the customer will get annoyed at the faceless organisation and will happily complain to teach you a good lesson.

Once you have approached your product with intent with the customer in mind, you'll find that customers will simply email you (because you've put your details on the box).

You can then move onto step two.

Have great support

Support is what all customers want. They want to know that if they have any issues, you'll be there, and you'll want to make it right.

Personally, the support of a company can completely change how I feel about their product. I can very quickly go from a fan of the brand and company to a complete hater to then boycotting them completely. This issue can be resolved so easily, yet many people completely overlook it. Here's how you do it in two steps:

- have easily accessible contact information;

- use the 'Acknowledge, Align, Assure' strategy.

HAVE EASILY ACCESSIBLE CONTACT INFORMATION

Pretty self-explanatory right? All you have to do here is have your contact details on the product packaging or a product insert that is EASILY accessible and not hidden in some fine print on the back of an instruction booklet. It can be small, that's fine – but not hidden, that's not fine. Laws may be different in your country, but as a rule of thumb, it's always best to have at minimum your business email and your registered business address along with company name and company number. Do not have brand@gmail.com. Instead, create a proper email like hello@mybrand.com If you have a product insert (just a card, piece of paper, or booklet) then be sure to clearly display your contact information there too and invite customers to email you with any concerns no matter how small.

In a moment, you are going to look at asking for reviews, part of this is reaching out to the customer first. This is so they have your email so they can easily respond to you with any questions or concerns.

USE THE ACKNOWLEDGE, ALIGN, ASSURE STRATEGY

If you've ever worked in customer service or in a customer-facing role, you should have already been taught this strategy or something like it. This strategy is a way to disarm an angry or upset customer within just a couple of sentences. It'll show them not only that you've heard their issue, but that you understand it and there is a resolution.

All customers want to be heard, and they just want the company to empathise with their situation. Also, they want a quick and efficient resolution so they can get on with their life. If you ever get any concerns, complains, issues, angry customers, or anything that isn't positive, use this three-step strategy.

1. ACKNOWLEDGE

This tells the customer that you've heard them and understand their issue.

For example:

Customer says: 'The product arrived, and within one week, it broke'.

You say: 'I understand that you've only just started

using the product, and it's broken within the first week.'

All you're doing is repeating back to them what they just told you. Not word for word, but in a conversational and normal way. This is so important as a customer wants to know that you understand their issue fully.

2. ALIGN

This allows you to empathise or sympathise with your customer's situation, so they know that you know how it feels.

For example:

Customer says: 'The product arrived, and within one week, it broke'.

You say: 'I can image how frustrated you are, no one likes it when something you've only just started using breaks so quickly'.

Or, you could say: 'I know exactly how you feel as I just had the same thing happen to me with a new [product] I just bought.'

This shows the customer that firstly, you're a human, not some cooperate drone just copy-and-pasting a response. It also shows the customer that you feel for their siltation as you're aligning their experience with one that you've had. This helps disarm the customer as then you're both on the same side rather than you being on the opposite side.

3. ASSURE

This is when you assure the customer that there is a resolution and where you can provide the resolution.

For example:

Customer says: 'The product arrived, and within one week, it broke'.

You say: 'Don't worry though, I assure you we'll get this resolved for you nice and quickly. I'm going to arrange for a replacement to be sent out to you ASAP free of charge.'

This now tells the customer what the resolution is in a way where they don't have to worry about it any longer. All you are trying to do with this strategy is to fix the issues as quickly as possible, but at the same time, you are making the customer feel good about it – like they are a valued customer and that you truly care about them and their experience.

What you'll find is that those customers that were super grumpy then will be the ones that turn around and actually apologise to you for being so short with you. They will commend you on your customer service, and, best of all, most of the time, they will leave 5-Star reviews!

Let's look at this all together as part of an actual reply:

Customer says: The product arrived, and within one week, it broke'.

You Email:

Hi there [Customer's Name],

I understand that you've only just started using [the product] and it's broken within the first week. Please first accept my sincerest apologies as this is the last thing I want.

I know exactly how you feel as I just had the same thing happen to me with some new headphones I just bought, but don't worry though, I assure you we'll get this quickly resolved for you.

I'm going to arrange for a replacement to be sent out to you ASAP free of charge. Are you able to confirm where you want it sent, e.g. the same address as before, or maybe a work address?

How does that sound?

If you have any questions, please do not hesitate to let me know.

Kind regards

[Your Name]

If any customers do not appreciate that response, then they are truly a miserable person and you can't help them. But for 99% of your customers, this response will be a breath of fresh air compared to the canned and personality lacking responses they are used to getting.

Those are the things you need to have first, but to actually get the reviews you need to ask for them! Very few customers will leave a review if unprompted. We all have busy lives and leaving a review for you isn't ever going to be on their to-do list.

ASKING FOR REVIEWS

Unprompted, the only reviews you'll get are the negative ones. People love a good old moan, and people love a good old moan even more online where they can sit at their keyboard furiously typing like their life depended on it. To combat this, you are going to use your exceptional customer service writing skills to persuade your customers to leave positive reviews and to contact you first with their negative experiences.

1 Dispatch → **2** 3 Days After Delivery → **3** 2 Days After Last Email → **4** 2 Days After Last Email

I use email follow-up sequences to achieve this. The follow-up is a sequence of four emails that are automatically sent to the customer upon specific triggers. These triggers are as follows:

- when the product is dispatched;

- three days after delivery;

- two days after the previous email;

- two days after the previous email.

I've tested variations of these emails, the times they are sent, the subject lines, and have put a great amount of time into these. It wouldn't be fair for me to just give away all my hard work and just let you copy and paste it right? Well as life isn't fair, I'm going to do exactly that.

Here are the exact emails I send in the follow-up sequence I use to get reviews. Feel free to take inspiration from them – or just steal them. Either is 100% okay.

Email 1: When the product is dispatched

Subject line: '😮 Super-secret information about your order...'

Message Body:

'Hi {{ Buyer First Name }},

Thank you for your recent purchase of your brand new HydroFuel™ Sports Water Bottle.

I just wanted to email you to let you know that your Bottle has been shipped and to also send you your **Hydro-Infused Fruit Infuser eBook** via email (attached). We've also added a Care Guide to the end of the eBook, be sure to check it out!

Our customers' satisfaction is our number one priority, so please let me know if there is **anything** that you can do to improve your experience. (We're not happy unless you're happy.)

In the meantime, feel free to track the progress of your order from this link: {{ Tracking Link:Tracking Link }}

Thank you again!

Amy

The HydroFuel Team'

Email 2: Three days after delivery

Subject Line: '📦 Did your next-door neighbour steal your parcel...'

Message Body:

'Hi Again {{ Buyer First Name }},

As it has been a few days since your HydroFuel Bottle arrived, I just wanted to check to make sure it arrived okay, in one piece, and exactly as expected.

As a small UK brand, I am competing against very large overseas companies, so I am following up on every order to make sure everything was delivered safe and sound.

Please let me know if there are any issues at all, and I will make sure to set things right

Our small team at HydroFuel works really hard to make our customers happy, from education and awareness to producing high quality, reliable, and eco-friendly products.

If you've got a moment, we'd love to hear your feedback. We'd also love it if you could include a picture!

{{ Product Review Link Stars }}

Best wishes,

Amy

The HydroFuel Team'

Email 3: Two days after previous email

Subject Line: '😀 Fancy A 15% Discount Code? '

Message Body:

'Hey {{ Buyer First Name }},

We again wanted to reach out and offer you a 15%-Off Discount Code if you'd like to purchase a brand new HydroFuel Bottle for any of your friends or family as a gift!

If you're interested, simply reply to this email letting us know, and we'll send you a code that you can use. No strings attached!

Selling on *Amazon* is what we do for a living to support ourselves, Product reviews are very important to the success of our business, but only a few customers leave them.

If you're HydroFuel Bottle made you happy ... and hydrated ... **it would mean the world to us if you could take just one minute to help share the love by leaving us an honest review.**

Even if you don't have time to spare to leave us a review, we still want to extend a big **THANK YOU** to you for helping our business grow!

{{ Product Review Link Stars }}

Thank you again for being one of our amazing customers!

Amy

The HydroFuel Team'

Email 4: 2 days after previous email

Subject Line: 'Don't keep it bottled up... 💧'

Message Body:

'Hey {{ Buyer First Name }},

By now you've had a good amount of time to try out your HydroFuel Bottle! I just wanted to check in one last time (I promise) and make sure everything went perfectly.

If you have any questions, issues, or would like the **15%-Off Discount Code for another one of our HydroFuel Bottles** I mentioned in my last email, please feel free to simply respond to this email letting me know, and I will personally get back to you ASAP!

If everything went as it was supposed to go and you ARE happy, it would be amazing and mean so much to us if you could spare one minute, click the stars below, and let us know about your experience.

{{ Product Review Link Stars }}

Thank you again. We really do appreciate it!

Amy

The HydroFuel Team'

There're a few key things I'd like to point out about these emails that really work to help conversions.

THE SUBJECT LINE:

This must be eye-catching. Test these subject lines in your inbox and see how you respond to them. A great tip is that next time you scroll through your inbox, just take note of what subject lines grab your attention and get you to open the email. Try adding an emoji but be careful not to overdo it.

Personally, I like to try and add a sense of light-heartedness to my emails and subject titles. This may help your customer form a bond with you and your brand, so they see you as approachable rather than a boring company that they see every day that probably won't listen.

ASK QUESTIONS

You are far more likely to get a response from an email if you ask a question. It seems silly when you think of it, but often companies just tell you information and never ask a question to solicit a response. If you can get a response, then you are one step closer to a 5-Star review, as now you can charm your customer and nurture them at every stage.

YOU AREN'T A LARGE COMPANY

Let the customer know that you're a small company just trying to create good products. Everyone loves local businesses, so lean into that and let your customers know more about you!

VALUE THE CUSTOMERS TIME

Getting a customer to do a review is a pain for them. It takes time out their day, so you better be extremely appreciative if a customer does go out their way to help you. They do not have any need to leave reviews. Doing so won't change their life one bit, so when you are asking for reviews, value the time of the customer.

ALWAYS HAVE A CALL-TO-ACTION AND LINK

What's the good in asking for a review but having no link to do so? Or equally, having a link to do so, but no instructions to click it? You have to have both. Always have a call-to-action and a clear way in which the customer can take the exact action that you want them to take.

SIGN OFF YOUR EMAIL

I do not know why this works, but when I started to sign off my emails as a girl rather than a guy, the replies got more numerous and the reviews did too. For all of you that are fortunate enough to not have to pretend to be someone you're not, then that's perfect. However, for me, I always sign off these emails as 'Amy', the customer support superhero that can defuse any situation.

Out of all of these, I believe the subject line has the most impact because if a customer doesn't notice your email, they won't click it, and if they don't click it, they cannot read it!

I get so many replies from this email sequence, especially to the second email where I ask about their neighbours stealing their parcel in the subject line. People love it, and it allows them to really picture it. I get customers tell me that they have really nice neighbours, and then I can tell them that they are lucky because mine are always up to no good. This creates an incredible rapport with your customers, so the more obscure and interesting you can make it, the better.

Try your hardest to create subject lines that create interest within your customers. You want to spike their interest, so they engage with your business. If you can do this, then you're onto a winning formula.

When you combine the three elements of incredible images, a fully, search-engine-optimised listing, and a tonne of killer reviews, you'll have yourself a listing that will really dominate over your competition. Do not underestimate how impactful these things are. Many sellers, not just on *Amazon* but all over the Internet, never put in enough effort, not because they don't want to put effort in, but because they have no idea of how the mind of a customer works.

Simply by reading this book and getting to this point, you're already ahead of 90% of the competition.

09

LAUNCHING YOUR PRODUCT INTO THE STRATOSPHERE

$$\boxed{\text{Launch}} = \left(\begin{array}{c} \text{Sales} \\ + \\ \text{7-Day Consistency} \end{array} \right)$$

T he best and simplest way to think about this is by using a rocket launch as an analogy. Maybe this is where a 'product launch' gets its name.

Why do you think a rocket needs to burn 11,000 pounds of fuel per second to take off? It's quite simple. It's because the rocket is firstly at standstill, its velocity is zero, and needs to get to around 17,600 mph to enter orbit which only takes around two to three minutes. The second reason is that it has the whole world is trying to pull it back down because of gravity.

So, to launch a rocket, you need to use fuel to increase velocity.

To launch a product, you need sales to increase your rank.

Before you start selling your product, it has zero sales and you want to get it to a point where it's generating 10, 20, 50, 100 sales a day, so, just like a rocket going into orbit. you need to fuel your product.

There are four types of fuel I like to use:

- reviews;

- PPC (Pay Per Click);

- giveaways;

- social media.

Just as a rocket needs to be going around 17,600 mph to enter orbit in around two to three minutes, to launch a product and get it ranked on page one for your search term, you need to have sales velocity plus at least a seven-day consistency.

HOW DO YOU CALCULATE HOW MANY SALES YOU NEED TO MAKE?

If your top competitors are doing 20 sales a day, then you need to be doing over 20 sales a day for around seven days, and you'll then rank above or close to them in the search results. The trick is knowing how to get these sales when previously you had zero customers.

REVIEWS

We've spoken about reviews and their importance, and this is never been truer than when launching a product. If you have zero reviews or even just a handful, it's just like having a rocket ship that's not finished. It launches, and soon after launch, it would blow up into a million pieces. Maybe not so catastrophic, however, there is no point going through the next three sections as if you don't have any reviews, then your product will quickly fail as potential customers do not trust it because of the lack of social proof.

Personally, I would look to get around 10+ reviews on your product before your official launch. However, be careful as there are various rules *Amazon* sets regarding reviews which, of course, change, so I would always check their terms of service to make sure you're aligning fully with them.

A misconception here is that a launch is when you sell your first product, however a launch is a date you choose at which point you'll put all your efforts into driving traffic to your listing. The pre-launch is when you can get a few sales and start getting reviews that you'll need for your official launch date.

We know how important images are to customers making buying decisions. An incredible strategy to help customers convert is to get images in the reviews. You'll notice in my email follow-up sequence, I actively ask customers to upload a photo with their review. What you must realise is that your first reviews on your product will probably be the most popular ones known as the 'top reviews'. So, you want to make sure they are thorough and not one-word reviews, and they have images attached to them.

Lastly, make sure that before you launch, your email sequence is live and ready to go, so when you start driving sales to your product on day-one of your seven-day launch, you have emails ready to be sent out immediately.

PPC (PAY PER CLICK)

Advertising makes the world go around. If there's one skill that I believe will make you successful in any business you have, it's knowing how to advertise. Fortunately for many you, most people are confused by advertising. They make mistakes and then claim, 'It doesn't work'. This is perfect as that's how you can stand out and make an impact!

'PPC' stands for 'Pay Per Click' advertising. This is exactly what it says on the tin. Every time a customer clicks on your advert, you pay. The terminology used can be confusing so before I move on I've picked out some of the most important terms you'll need to understand.

BID

A bid, or a keyword bid, is the amount you're willing to

pay for a customer to click on your advert. Think of this like an *eBay* auction where the higher you bid, the more likely you are to win the auction.

BUDGET

Your budget is how much you're willing to spend on any particular day. If you set a budget of £10 per day, then you will spend no more than £10 in that day.

AUTOMATIC CAMPAIGN

This is where *Amazon* will use their algorithm to place bids on relevant keywords based upon the data it has about your listing.

MANUAL CAMPAIGN

A manual campaign is when you are telling *Amazon* exactly what keywords to bid on and how much to bid. You are in control of all variables.

EXACT MATCH

An 'exact match' keyword is where you create a bid for a keyword, and to show the advert, a customer would have to search for that exact keyword or phrase. For example, if the keyword you entered into your campaign was, 'wireless headphones', then that advert will only show to customers that search for 'Wireless Headphones' and not for any other keywords or keyword phrases.

BROAD MATCH

A 'broad match' keyword is where you add the keyword,

and then *Amazon* will show your advert to searches that are similar, related to, or synonyms for the keyword that you entered. For example, if you entered 'wireless headphones', your ads might show for customers that type in, 'wireless earphones' / 'Bluetooth headphones' / 'over ear headphones', etc.

PHRASE MATCH

This is where *Amazon* will add keywords before and/ or after the keyword you enter to create a phrase. Also, they would not split up your keyword. For example, if you used 'wireless headphones', *Amazon* would not add in a keyword between 'wireless' and 'headphones', but they would add in keywords before and after, for example, 'black wireless headphones for men'.

PLACEMENTS

A placement is defining where your advert is shown. All advertising platforms will have these, as ads are shown in different places. On *Amazon*, you can show up not only for search but also on other sellers' listings that are similar to yours. So, not only can you have your ad shown when customers search for a product, but you can have your advert shown directly on your competitions' listing.

When I'm asked, 'What type of campaigns do you run – broad, phrase, exact, placements, etc.?' My answer is simple, 'You want to run all of them.'

When starting out. you need to gather data, so you know actually how customers are searching, what ads convert to sales, and what ads are not converting to a sale. The more data you have, the better you can optimise your advertising campaigns. This is why you always start with Automatic campaigns and Broad- and Phrase-matching campaigns as this allows *Amazons'* advanced algorithms to show your ads to relevant customers. Once you have a couple of weeks' worth of data, you can then optimise. This is the simplest way I can explain how to do this.

- every week get an export of your advertising results

- find keywords that are converting profitably

- make a note of them including your bid for that keyword.

- create an exact match campaign

- Target the converting keywords at the bid you know is profitable

- over time adjust the bid to see if lowering or increasing it will drive more or less sales

- make a list of all the keywords that are costing you money and not making sales

- add them to the 'Negative Keyword' field. (this tells *Amazon* that you do not want your ads showing to customers that search for that keyword).

The combination of focusing on the keywords that do convert and removing the ones that don't is the key to optimising your campaigns.

To finesse the optimisation over time, you will be adjusting the bids on the keywords to find the 'Goldilocks Zone' for each keyword where it is providing the most sales possible per day at the most profitable cost. Of course, it is important to learn how to do this yourself, however once you have your system set up and it's working, I would advise you to hire a freelancer that can spend a few hours each week optimising your ad campaigns to reduce ACOS (Average Cost of Sales) and to increase revenue.

You may think that this will cost a lot, but you can get this from around $5 to $10 per hour. To get the best value for your money, I use a website called upwork.com. You create a job, and freelancers will apply for the job. You can then screen them and hire them. All payments are done through Upwork so both you and the freelancer are protected. My tips for finding freelancers is to create a job with a small budget, around $5 an hour and up to five hours per week. By doing this, you will push away all the freelancers based in the UK, US, etc., as they generally will not work for this amount. However, you will open up applications from places where the average living wage is significantly less, therefore, the $5 is proportionally worth more to them.

The common misconception when I tell people how I do this is that surely, if you pay them less, they do a worse job. This couldn't be further from the truth. In fact, some on my best freelancers are based in India, the Philippines, and Brazil. They all do incredible work, maintain an extremely high standard, and all have an incredible work ethic. The key is that you have to check their previous work and make sure, like any freelancer, it's good!

By doing it this way, you can save yourself three to four hours a week of optimisation and only have to give up $30-50 of profit. For me, this is a no-brainer!

GIVEAWAYS

Doing product giveaways is my least favourite method to get initial sales because you're giving away valuable stock. A giveaway is where you create deep discounts on your products so that they are just a couple of pounds, meaning that they are an easy sell as the cost is far lower than the value of the product. You can use services like *Viral Launch* among others to do this, but I would approach your launch by only using giveaways as an option as part of your strategy to rank. With only using giveaways, you have to give an undesirable amount of stock away for next to nothing.

The idea is that *Amazon* sees a sale as a sale rather than how much is being made from the sale. So, if you are doing 20 sales a day from giveaways (20 close-to-free units), then *Amazon* sees this as you're making 20 sales. If your competition is only doing 15 a day, then you're likely to rank above them in the search results. Of course, giving away 20 units a day over a minimum of a 7-day window, you'll be giving away around 140 units.

While I do condone the use of giveaways, I would have them as an additional tool you can use to add to the launch success.

SOCIAL MEDIA

Using social media can be a critical asset to your business, not just at launching phase, but throughout the lifecycle of the product or business. The other strategies can be done fairly quickly, however setting up and building a social media following, or using adverts, is a longer-term plan and will take longer to create. However, the upside to social media is not just the fact that you can gain very broad exposure if done correctly, but for the most part, its 100% free!

I could write a whole book just on social media, and maybe I will, however for this section, I want to go over the three main focus areas for you launching a product:

- building social platforms;
- offering discounts;
- leveraging influencers.

BUILDING SOCIAL PLATFORMS

The beauty of social media is that most platforms are free to use which is great for you as you can get free exposure for your company. Before starting, I would always focus on one social media platform as your 'main' platform, then have the others that support the first. For example, I have my *YouTube* channel, which is my main platform for delivering content, and then I have *Facebook* mainly used for community and support, and *Instagram* for day-to-day updates. Each platform has a unique use which makes them great to better understand where your customers are hanging out online.

If they are searching on *YouTube*, then that's where you want your brand to be. If they are in *Facebook* groups, then that's where you want to be. Find your customers and then create a social media presence around the platform they use on a daily basis. Think of it like this, would you post pictures of your home accessories on your professional *LinkedIn* account? Of course you wouldn't, as the audience isn't the right one. So, before you start creating loads of different accounts, first think about what platform is best for you.

OFFERING DISCOUNTS

Now that you've built a social media following, you can start to introduce that you're launching a product. You can start capturing emails in lead-up to the launch by offering a discount code. People love a good discount, and if you've done a good job at growing a targeted, social media following, then these people should jump at the chance to get a discount on a product they would clearly want.

I would recommend you set up a simple website where you can capture the customer's email address. This is so you can send them the discount code and link when you launch, but also you can market to the customer via email for free! Do not underestimate your email list, and giving discounts is great way to get them.

You might be thinking that I just said doing giveaways isn't ideal. The good thing about building a social presence is that you can give a launch discount of 50%, break even so that you can drive sales, and not lose any money on fulfilment fees! Simply work out your break-even cost, then you know exactly how much you'll be willing to give away when the time comes.

In conclusion, the key with your product launch is to focus all your efforts to drive as many sales as possible within a seven-day window so that you can start to rank on *Amazon.* As soon as you have ranked for your main keywords and you have a high-converting product listing, you'll start to get organic sales.

A couple of notes before I move on. Firstly, if you don't have a high-converting listing, it may be a lot harder to maintain your position, however if you follow the lessons taught in this book, you're going to be ahead of most sellers out there. Secondly, when you go to launch, pick a date once your stock is at *Amazon*'s warehouse, you have some reviews, and everything is set to go. Don't think that as soon as your stock is sellable you need to go and launch the same day. Take your time and get it right ... once.

10

HOW TO GO FROM A FIVE, TO A SIX, TO A SEVEN FIGURE COMPANY

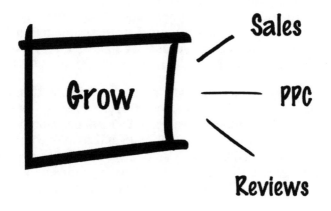

When I first started, I had goals of making just an extra £500 per month, and at the time, that seemed like a life-changing amount – and it was for me back then. For a long time, I was hungry to get to the magic £10,000-per-month landmark, and I was pushing forward relentlessly for this. It took quite a few months to get to that point but after hitting that £10K and just a couple months after that I was hitting £20,000 per month just 6 months later, I was doing over £60,000 in just 30 days.

What on earth happened? How did I go from making nothing to making tens of thousands of pounds each month?

The key to all of this was that I focused on progression, moving forward and not looking back. I reinvested money back into my companies rather than letting it just build up. But what you realise soon after making these amounts is that it's not about the money. For me, it's about the progression and the impact that money can make.

For you at the moment, you may be reading this, and you're at zero looking to get to £1,000 per month. You may be at £10,000 and looking to get to £50,000 per month. You have to learn how to use your time and money wisely so that one day you can use the money to buy the things you want, to give to the causes you believe in, and generally do whatever you want with both your time and your money.

HOW DO YOU GO FROM A FIVE- TO A SIX- TO A SEVEN-FIGURE COMPANY?

Like the foundations of a house, you probably won't get to six and seven figures unless you have solid foundations. For us, this will be having a good product, understanding your customers, and creating an incredible experience for them. If you have these foundations, then scaling becomes far easier. If you're at the point where you're scratching your head as to how to improve your foundations, then maybe you've missed a few chapters. I'd consider re-reading the book!

Let's assume you all have taken these lessons on board and wanting to scale. There are really just 4 steps to growing your business:

- reinvesting profits;

- optimisation;

- more customers;

- more products.

REINVESTING PROFITS

Albert Einstein is said to have called it *'the most powerful force in the universe.'* He was talking about the power of compounding. Your goal is to scale your business, and to do that, you need to buy more stock to sell. To buy more stock, you need more money. You get that money from your profits. If you were to not reinvest that profit and use it for something else, then you simply don't have the money to buy more stock. .The knock-on effect is that if you don't reinvest your profits, you'll have a smaller amount to use for future profits, and this compounds over time.

So, let's do the math ...

Example:

Reinvesting your full 30% profit margin:

- your landed cost is £2 per unit, and the product sells for £10.

- the first order you buy 500 units costing £1,000.

- you sell all 500 units and make £5,000 in sales.

- at 30% profit, you make £1,500 profit, and you get back your £1,000 you initially invested.

Now, you have (£1,500 + £1,000) £2,500.

- with this £2,500, you can afford to buy 1,250 units at £2 each which will generate £12,500 in sales with a profit of £3,750.

- adding on your initial stock investment of £2,500 you now have **£6,250**.

OR ...

If you reinvested just 10% of your profits over the same cycle of orders for three stock orders, you would have just **£3,375** compared to **£6,250** if you had reinvested 30% rather than 10%. That's around twice as much money available for growing your company. This is only after three reinvestment cycles. Imagine what it would get to after ten or twenty reinvestment cycles!

This is how you go from investing just a few thousand at the start to making hundreds of thousands in the future.

When you're considering taking money out your company for paying for a holiday or buying new Gucci trainers, just think about how much you could make that money into if you just reinvested it back into your company. I'm not saying don't enjoy your money. All I'm saying is be aware of what happens to your growth potential when you start spending instead of re-investing.

OPTIMISATION

We've spoken about attention spans earlier in this book, and I told you about a story where my friend was swiping through *Tinder* at astonishing rates.

There's actually a lot you can learn from *Tinder*, as without knowing it, for anyone that uses it, they are normally, constantly working on their optimisation. There are a few areas you can edit such as the images and the bio section, and as anyone that uses *Tinder* or any dating app will know, these are crucial to a successful ... I was going to say 'love life', however, I think ... 'hook-up' is probably better suited. You may simply change your first image on your profile, and you may get better or worse results. If you get less interest, then the picture isn't as good, right?

Selling on *Amazon* and scaling on *Amazon* are just as shallow. So, how do you continue to optimise over time to get more 'hook-ups'?

We optimise everything!

Not just your images, but your SEO, your advertising, your listing copy, applying for brand registry, adding variations, and a lot more ... Your goal is to get the highest-converting-product listing possible, and unfortunately this takes time. In fact, I advise people only make one or two changes and then track the results for one to two weeks before making a decision as to if it's worked or not. The reason why I say make only a small number of changes is that you need to be able to monitor what exactly worked and what didn't. If you go changing everything and your conversions decrease, then how do you know what caused the drop off? However, if you've only made one change, you know that it'll be down to that so you can back it out and try something else.

Some people don't actually track the results which is madness. When you make a change like editing your first image or making a PPC change, then you need to be able to monitor it and have tangible results to reflect upon. Let the numbers do the talking, and if after two weeks the numbers are telling you that it's working, keep that change. If the numbers tell you that it's not working, go back to the original, but only if the data tells you that.

Quite often sellers will make a change, and the next day the sales shoot up and they email me saying, 'OMG, this is amazing!' However, that spike in sales can be completely unrelated to the change they made. The next day, they could have the worst day they've ever had and then think that the changes didn't work. All these ups and downs can really mess with your decision making. Instead, what you need to do is look at the change over a longer period of time as sales throughout the week will fluctuate due to things in and out of your control. After two weeks, you can compare the week-on-week differences, and then you can make an informed decision as to if the changes had a positive or negative impact.

Remember, let the numbers do the talking!

Here are some of the things you may want to optimise.

FIRST IMAGE (HERO IMAGE)

Create variations of your first image, use the experiment I showed you earlier in the book first, then once you have created what you think to be a more eye-catching image, replace the one you have and see if it helps the click-through rate. This can be literally the make-or-break change because if you're getting clicks, then those clicks will turn into sales and money in your pocket.

THE REST OF THE IMAGES

Always be thinking about how you can communicate the benefits of your product in a more concise way to your customers. Check into your competition and see what they're doing as they may have identified a benefit that you have in the product but don't promote so you'll want to make sure your customers know you also have it!

PPC

Optimising your advertising will be where most of your time is spent. The goal is to reduce your ACOS and increase your spend so you can be as profitable as possible while also scaling. I recommend that you do this once a week. This gives you enough time to gather data and make informed decisions. I'd also consider outsourcing this to a PPC expert that'll be able to spend a few hours a week doing it for you, then send you the report at the end of the week. This will really save you an enormous amount of time so you can focus on other things.

VARIATIONS

A great way to optimise your listing is to add product variations like size, colour, and material. If you sell a product that can be purchased in different sizes, but you only sell one size, then you are cutting off large revenue streams from customers that want to other sizes. When possible, always look at how you can add variations to your listing so your customers have more buying options but be careful not to give too much unnecessary choice as a confused customer doesn't buy.

EMAIL FOLLOW UPS

Something as simple as a subject line can completely change how effective your email sequence is in getting reviews. A great tip for this is every time you get an email that makes you stop and read it, think about what part the subject line made you stop, and think about what you can learn from it. If you can optimise how many customers open your emails and read them, it'll have a direct impact on your reviews, and your reviews will have a direct impact on your sales.

SEO

Personally, I don't like to mess around with SEO that often, however, every couple of months, it's a good idea to do some research on your main keywords just to see if there are any new keywords that customers are searching for that you didn't know about. Be careful not to make too many changes. Do one section at a time. For example, change one bullet point or part of your description or title. Get the feedback from the results and make decisions based off your data.

BRAND REGISTRY

If you've ever been on *Amazon* and seen a seller that has a description full of images and nice bullet points, it is because they have enrolled in *Amazon*'s Brand Registry program which allows them to add Enhanced Brand Content to their listing. Not all sellers get this, but it's a great tool to be able to add more images and more information about your product. Since not everyone has it, it'll set you apart from the other sellers and increase your conversions. You must have an active trademark for your brand to be able to be approved.

These are just a few of the ways that you're going to

want to start optimising going forward, and if you fail to do so, you'll be leaving a considerable amount of money on the table for your competitors to take. You want to optimise every step of the customer's journey from searching for a product to buying to leaving reviews, and to promoting to friends, and so on ... At every stage, you'll be able to optimise something to get more clicks, more sales, and more reviews. Even if it's on a 0.2% change in the right direction, it's a change you'll want to keep, as the higher rate you convert, the more money you'll make, the more you'll be able to reinvest, and the more successful you'll eventually be.

If you're currently selling and you're not optimising, you're literally shooting yourself in the foot as a competitor will beat you to it, and you'll be then left chasing your tail wondering why you didn't focus on it more when you could.

MORE CUSTOMERS

The issue with a lot of brick-and-mortar shops is that they have geographical limits that prevent them from scaling, or they have constraints with the size of their shop. Think about your local hairdresser. They are limited by how many seats they have, how many hours they are open, and how many customers will travel to them on a daily basis. This creates a ceiling beyond which they just cannot scale. After they reach capacity, all they can do is up their price or move premises.

For you, you have the mighty power of *Amazon* behind you with millions of customers and almost limitless warehouse space. Your hurdle is just about finding more customers, and to get more customers, it's actually very simple – not easy – but simple.

For more customers to buy your product, more customers have to know that it exists. It's really as simple as that. The more people know about it, the more people buy it.

SO HOW DO YOU GET MORE CUSTOMERS?

Firstly, you want to get as big a market share as possible within your current platforms. So, if you're primarily selling on *Amazon*, you want to do everything to increase your rank so you show up higher for more keywords and therefore get more customers. You do this through the optimisation I just spoke about and really leverage PPC to get in front of more customers eyes.

The second is that you can start to look for sales off of *Amazon* or on a different platform. Many people still don't use *Amazon* to shop, but they are buyers. It's just they don't yet know about your product. You can look into using your own website to promote using paid advertising or social media influencers to find more customers. A great tip for seeing what's possible is by simply Googling the product and searching for brands on *Facebook*. You can quickly see who is running ads, and then you can then visit their website and see everything they are doing. Just approach it as if you were a customer and take notes on what they do, how they price their products, and if you really want to understand their process, buy the product from them, and then you can see behind the curtain and get to see what emails they send and how they handle customer issues.

MORE PRODUCTS

I ask people all the time, 'How many products do you think Apple sell?' Often, the response I get is '500? 5,000?' and so on. However, you'll be really surprised to find out that actually they really only have five products – what they call their 'hero products':

- iPhone;
- iPad;

- iMac;

- MacBook;

- Apple Watch

They also then add on 'services' to the list.

The point is that they put a lot of focus onto a handful of products, whereas the likes of Samsung pretty much sell any technology device you can think of from phones to washing machines. Yet Apple, selling a fraction of the number of products, make substantially more money and was the first company valued at $1T. The way they're able to dominate is by having a huge focus on just a small number of things meaning more care and attention goes into those products and results in a better customer experience. Then, once you have a good product that's clearly better than the competition, your customers will do the promoting for you.

Most *Amazon* sellers take the Samsung approach, just release product after product, not really making any of them stick. They never become a best seller or even close to it by having to put in more work to maintain all of those products. I want you to take the Apple approach and focus on one product at a time. Once you've mastered that product, you can replicate that success with another product as you now know how to really dominate with just one product. Some of my best students are killing it because they don't rush into adding to their product line. They understand that greatness takes time, and it's better to have one product making £20,000 per month than having 10 products making £20,000 total, as you'll have 10 times less work to do. You may think that it's harder that way around, but in fact, it's easier as you can have laser focus on just one thing at a time. If you do this, your results will be extraordinary. To scale using more products, focus on replicating success rather than throwing products out there and seeing what sticks.

Just go one product at a time, and not before long you'll have your five 'hero products' bringing you large amounts every month.

In summary, growing your business is key to its long-term success, and being able to reinvest into your business is one of the most influential ways to scale – but don't ever forget about optimisation and improving your service or product offering. This is exactly how some of my most successful students have gone on to create six-figure companies within the space of literally a few months, and how they will go on to create and run multi-million-pound businesses in the future.

CONCLUSION

All good things have to come to an end, and this does mark the end of this book, however the learning will not end here. I will not go quietly into the night.

You've just consumed a considerable amount of information that has taken me years to collect and perfect, so don't be put off if you have to go back and re-read sections. Actually, some of my favourite books, I re-read once a year as there's always things you miss a second or even a third time around. I promise you that if you fully grasp and take on board the teaching in this book, it'll change your life forever with whatever business you decide to go into. However, every giant leap starts with a small step, so take action today so you can change your life tomorrow.

I wish, I mean I *really* wish I had this book when I first started. The issue with the online world at the moment is everywhere you turn you get new and conflicting information, and after a while, you get information overload. Take some time to focus on just one thing, one trainer, one support system, and take advantage of it rather than trying to get your finger into all the pies. The whole ethos of this book and my strategy is to have a special focus on one thing, as with this special focus comes the best results.

I really hope I've been able to serve you and add a lot of value to your life with this book. I've given you some of the most advanced insights into how to really stand out. The only reason you'll fail is if you don't take action. You have to make the decision to be successful. Nothing will happen without you jumping in with both feet.

Remember, you're just one product away ...

Jonny Bradley

THE SELLERPRO ACADEMY

I f you've just finished reading this book and you're pumped to learn more and want my help, then I have a lot more to show you. I could fill a library with all the information I've built up, and the One Product Strategy is really just the tip of the iceberg.

For those of you that know me already, you'll know that I have a full training program and support structure called the SellerPro Academy. Since launching it, I have grown incredibly quickly, not because I do most of the marketing (which I don't), but because the value provided is the highest quality in the world. You then couple that with the best support and community in the world – basically all the things I wish I had when I started.

Since launching the Academy, I have created so many incredible success stories, and in 2018, I introduced the 10K Club Award. In 2019, I launched the 100K Club award. They represent an incredible landmark is each recipients journey. You can see these results and hear what they have to say at www.sellerproacademy.com/success-wall.

It's my mission to help you change your life, one product at a time. So, as many of you as possible reach the 10K and 100K Club, achieve your goals, change your life, and ultimately say, 'I did it!'

With hours' worth of video tutorials, countless resources, scripts, specialist support, mastermind groups, accountability chat, incubator, product consultants, and much, much more, the SellerPro Academy is for those people that are wanting to take action fast, to get the quickest and most efficient results without cutting any corners.

I'd actually like to invite you to join us and become part of our incredible community.

You can join us today at www.sellerproacademy.com

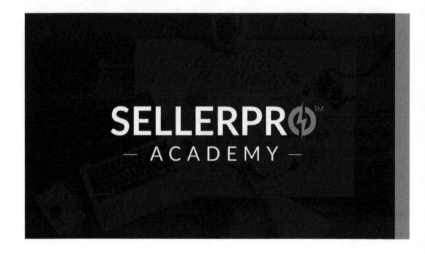

ACKNOWLEDGEMENTS

This book has been a long time coming, even if I didn't actually know it. Whilst everyone would love to claim that they did it themselves, I owe a big debt to those that have helped me along the way.

I would never normally thank a company, however there is one company that helped me become who I am today and that's Apple. By extension I must acknowledge all my colleagues that I worked with side by side for the best part of five years; you helped mould me into the person I am today to be the best version of myself. Apple was where I crafted my skills as a mentor, as a people person and as someone who values connection above all else.

Moving on from my professional career, I started looking into selling on *Amazon* and I had one shining light of confidence always pushing me forward. His name is Anhwa Griffiths. I truly believe that if it wasn't for him pushing me every day to get selling, make more videos, and hustle harder, I wouldn't be sitting here today writing this book. For nearly 30 days straight, Anhwa told me to quit my job, even though I was really not in the position to do so. The incredible thing is that because I had that fire being lit underneath me, it helped me take the actions needed to quit my job on the 30th day.

Nearly every day I'm calling up Jordan Platten, a fellow entrepreneur, for advice, or he is calling me. I met Jordan at Apple where I trained him and knew I'd get along with him because of his entrepreneurial spirit. Over the past two years in building my businesses, It was key to have someone like Jordan there for support, to call me out on my stupid ideas, to praise the great ones and to, of course, have a good laugh. Times can get really hard as an entrepreneur, and I'm so grateful to have Jordan there to support me.

Thanks must also go to some of the influential people on my team that helped make this book a reality.

I must thank William Richards, who is responsible for the majority of all the design and marketing for not only the One Product Strategy but for all of my businesses. His dedication to put in the long hours and to not accept average-quality work is so influential in the success of everything we've been able to create.

Gary White is a master when it comes to funnels. He not only creates beautiful websites but also, he understands my customers on a deep level, understanding what they will and will not like. Many times, I've run ideas by Gary for him to shut them down almost immediately. If Gary wasn't around to help me, I'd have made some really silly mistakes!

Content creation is incredibly time-consuming which is why thanks must go to Dan Prior who has supported me from nearly the beginning. He is one of those people that sees a problem and finds the resolution. There was never an issue too big for Dan to tackle.

When writing this book, I wanted only the best to evaluate it, that's why I'd love to thank Julie Eason and Julie Willson for their dedication and attention to detail in evaluating this book. I can assure you that it wouldn't be half as good as it is if they hadn't have been involved.

Last, a massive thank you to my partner, Sophie, and our families whose support I count upon and couldn't do without. You all have incredible patience to be able to put up with my constant shenanigans, my shiny-object syndrome, and my short attention span.

There are, of course, many others that helped me,

gave their support and feedback, and to all of you, I'm tremendously grateful.

Thank you all!

Jonny

Contents

BIBLIOGRAPHY

Bureau of Labor Statistics' Business Employment Dynamics, N.D. Survival of private-sector establishments by opening year, Viewed 29 July 2019, <https://www.bls.gov/bdm/us_age_naics_00_table7.txt>

Encyclopaedia Britannica, Inc., May 10, 2019, Uncertainty principle, Viewed 30 July 2019, <https://www.britannica.com/science/uncertainty-principle>.

Sedniev, Andrii. The Business Idea Factory. CreateSpace Independent Publishing Platform, November 7, 2013. Print

USA Today, Marco della Cava, September 19, 2013, Jony Ive: The man behind Apple's magic curtain, Viewed 30 July 2019, <https://www.usatoday.com/story/tech/2013/09/19/apple-jony-ive-craig-federighi/2834575/>.

Warren Berger, A More Beautiful Question, N.D. The Power Of "Vuja De", Viewed 20 July 2019, <http://amorebeautifulquestion.com/power-of-vuja-de/>.

GLOSSARY

ACOS - ADVERTISING COST OF SALE -

It is a key metric used to gauge the performance of your Amazon PPC campaigns. It indicates the ratio of ad spend to targeted sales and is calculated by a formula. ACoS = ad spend : sales.

Amazon Fulfilment Fee - This is the fee you pay for using Amazon to fulfill your orders once a customer has placed an order with your product. It is usually based on size and weight of the products you sell. It covers the cost for order picking, packing, shipping, and inner packaging.

ASIN - Amazon Standard Identification Number. A 10-character alphanumeric unique identifier assigned by Amazon and its partners for product identification.

Bid - PPC Bids is a way to pay for the advertisements that many people see on the search engine results page. The ads that PPC bids pay for are called sponsored links or sponsored ads and appear when certain keywords that the PPC bid purchased is entered into the search query. There are keywords that draw higher PPC bids.

Example: Your campaign generated you £250 in sales with an ad expenditure of £60 over a certain period of time. Your ACoS = 60 / 250 = 24%. You are spending roughly a quarter on ads to make £1 of sales with the campaign.

Class - A class is a classification of the product type for a trademark.

Customs Duty - It is a tariff or tax imposed on goods when transported across international borders. The purpose of customs duty is to protect each country's economy and domestic industries from more efficient or predatory competitors from abroad. Customs duty rates will vary from each product.

DDP - Delivery Duty Paid. A delivery agreement whereby the seller assumes all responsibility, risk, and costs associated with the goods until the buyer receives or transfers the goods to the destination port.

EORI - European Union Registration and Identification number. Used for businesses which import goods from outside the EU. A way to track and declare goods going into customs.

FBA - Short abbreviation for "Fulfilled By Amazon."

FBM - Fulfilled by Merchant - This allows you to store and ship your inventory yourself instead of Amazon. You have the advantage to maintain all inventory. This can lower costs because Amazon's fees are based on the size of the item. This is especially true for items that have a slower turn rate.

FOB - Free On Board / Freight On Board Responsibility is split fairly equal between the seller and buyer of goods. The FOB terms are the supplier's responsibility for paying all the costs involved with your shipment until it reaches the nearest port. Once the products are loaded onto the vessel (e.g., ship), the responsibility is shifted to you as the buyer for any costs and risks involved in the onward shipment. You need a freight forwarder to continue delivery to Amazon warehouse. FOB should include a reference to a port also, e.g., FOB Shanghai. Costs also vary from port to port and are not always closest to the seller due to high costs.

Hazmat - Dangerous goods with hazardous materials or simply "hazmat." Product contains materials that may pose a risk to health, safety, property, or the environment while storing, handling, or transporting. Hazmats may contain flammable, pressurised, corrosive, or otherwise harmful substances.

HTML - Hypertext Markup Language It's a standard web system for tagging text files to achieve font, colour, graphics, and hyperlink effects on web pages.

MOQ - Minimum Order Quantity. Some suppliers require a minimum quantity of the product to be ordered to meet their pricing figures. This figure does not need to be taken too seriously. It is just a guideline.

Niche - Relating products, services, interests to appeal to a small population mass of people. E.g., "Sports" – products will revolve around the sports niche.

OESP - Owned Emotional Selling Point - The emotional selling point attributed to a brand that is used to relate to the customer's emotions.

Patents - A government authority or license confirming a right or title for a set period of time. It has the sole right to exclude others from using, making, or selling an invention. Essentially it is intellectual property that prohibits from others using it, protecting the idea behind the product.

PPC - Price Per Click. Your online advertising model in which you pay each time a user clicks on one of the ads. There are various PPC ads, but the most common type is the paid-search ad. They appear when people search for things using a search engine such as Google, especially commercial searches with the potential to purchase.

Reverse ASIN - Amazon Standard Information Number. Amazon's internal tracking to identify for each listing in their catalog. It's similar to a UPC but exclusive to Amazon.

Seller Central - The portal that Amazon sellers use to list, maintain, and see an overview of their product's performance on. It is also a place for help and resources.

SEO - Search Engine Optimisation - is the strategy, techniques, and tactics used to increase the amount of visitors to a website by obtaining a high-ranking placement in the search results page of a search engine.

SKU - Stock Keeping Unit. A number assigned to a product to identify price, product options, and manufacturer of a product.

USP - Unique Selling Point - A feature or characteristic of a product, service, etc., that distinguishes it from others

VAT - Value Added Tax, known in some countries as a "Goods and Services Tax" (GST). VAT is collected by the end retailer and is usually a flat-tax rate. VAT is based on the increase in value of a product or service at each stage of production or distribution.

Understanding the Seven Churches of Revelation

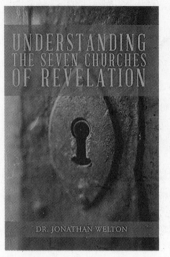

What little has been written about the seven letters to the churches in Revelation tends to utilize the lens of interpretation called dispensationalism. But the book itself gives us no indication that the letters to the churches are anything but letters to churches in the first century. In this unique book, Jonathan Welton applies the historical-contextual method of hermeneutics to these letters, which begins with the questions *who, where, when, what*, and *why*.

Jonathan delves deeply into the historical context of each individual letter for excellent, but often hidden insight. Since church history tells is that each of these churches was a literal historical church (not a metaphor, as dispensationalism proposes) John was addressing specific situations relevant to each church during the first century. When we look at the historical and cultural dynamics of the cities, we find that the letters are, in fact, very specific and unique to the historic reality.

Says the author:
"I have read other historically thorough sources, and I have done my own research, including traveling to and touring the modern locations of each of the seven churches mentioned in chapters 2 and 3 of the book of Revelation. In doing so, I have discovered an incredible list of connections between the cultural, geographical and historical events of the first century in these cities and the contents of Jesus' letters to them. I've written the book I wish I had read when I was seventeen and eager to understand what these beautiful yet cryptic letters were all about. I believe these letters hold significant and relevant information that influences our understanding of this book as a whole and that holds practical relevance for our lives."

New Age Masquerade

By far this is the most unique book regarding the New Age Movement from a Christian perspective. Jonathan Welton reveals the history of the New Age Movement from Swedenborgism to the modern New Age, while demonstrating that each of the movements leaders originally had roots within Christianity. The New Age isn't a Christian movement, but it is a movement away from a Christian foundation.

Other Topics covered:

- What is the difference between a Christian and a New Ager?
- Are we to have showdowns like Elijah vs the Prophets of Baal?
- How do we discern the counterfeit from the authentic?

Are you curious about what the Bible says about: The Age of Aquarius, the silver cord, necromancy, the Zodiac, ESP, Automatic writing, ectoplasm, and zombies? This book is for you!

From the Foreword by Patricia King

"Jonathan Welton has done a tremendous job writing *New Age Masquerade*. In it, he brilliantly discloses the biblical foundations that have been counterfeited in specific New Age practices. The enemy has take Scriptural truth, twisted it, and dangled it before the spiritually hungry. He knows all people were created for encounter with God, and his goal is to draw people away from Jesus and unto himself.

"Remember, if there is a counterfeit, there must be an authentic. In *New Age Masquerade*, Jonathan will introduce you to the authentic."

Additional Material by Dr. Jonathan Welton

UNDERSTANDING THE WHOLE BIBLE
The King, The Kingdom, and the New Covenant

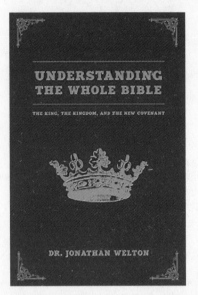

This textbook is the distillation of a nineteen-week course, Understanding the Whole Bible from Genesis to Revelation taught by author and theologian Dr. Jonathan Welton. If you want to devour the Word, this textbook will give you the knife, fork and even tuck in your napkin and teach you how to eat! Topics include: - Learn the difference between Systematic and Biblical Theology - How did we get our Bible? - Translations and study tools - Freewill versus Predestination - Dispensationalism and Covenant Theology - Cessationism and Supernaturalism - The Five Major Covenants: Noah, Abraham, Moses, David, and the New Covenant - The Covenant Promises fulfilled - God is not an Old Covenant monster - Understanding the At-One-Ment - Better Covenant Theology - The Great Covenant Transition - The End of Age - The Unveiling of Jesus - The One Law of the New Covenant World.

What others have said:

This is an instant classic. 'A book that shows the Bible is the story of God's covenant journey with His people.' Dr. Jonathan Welton has presented one of the most comprehensive and revelatory books on the King, the Kingdom, and the New Covenant.

Jonathan Welton has shifted my entire understanding of the Bible and his book provides so much clarity on what the Bible really is saying. Seeing Scripture through the lens of the covenants is so needed and many miss this vital perspective.